Praise for

Beneath the Surface

This memoir walks readers through a life of trauma and of healing. It's evident to the reader that this was a cathartic experience for the author. These stories deserve to be told, and many people will resonate with them. It is detailed and yet remarkably succinct. Rob captures the reality that facing the past is difficult *and* worth it when the time is right. He normalizes the experience of feeling chained to the past, the regret that comes with painful moments, and the hope to continue on. I recommend this memoir to anyone working through their own pain or trying to understand the pain of another.

—Julie Bates-Maves, PhD, LPC

Beneath the Surface shows us that it is possible to rewrite one's story. It challenges the reader to move through the pain, shift their perspective, find how the tragedies of childhood made them who they are, and embrace the gifts that arose from the darkness. The lessons learned are impactful, and *Beneath the Surface* is a must read for anyone ready to begin their own healing journey.

—Michelle Markquart, Founder and
Executive Director, Eau Claire Sober Living

This profound and moving memoir is not just a story of personal triumph, it is an inspiring guide offering hope to anyone seeking to overcome their own struggles, reminding us that true healing comes from facing our problems. A beautifully written testament to the enduring human spirit, it will resonate deeply with anyone who reads it.

—Dr. Stacey Bean, MD, MA,
Dual Certified Gestaltist,
Functional Medicine Practitioner at
Indigo & Sage Functional Wellness, LLC

Beneath the Surface is a deep dive into a personal path to wholeness. Rob reminds us that transformation and healing are available when we are ready, and that we can become our own life's hero. The lessons he provides are life-changing and timeless wisdom.

—Marsha Bressack, Life Coach,
Heart and Soul Centered Coaching

Robert's life is a very powerful story of trials and tribulations. I felt like I was in the room during his negative experiences but also by his side as he broke the surface of dark negativity and found the light that has led him to his successes. Each one of us must endure challenges and Robert's life has not been exempt from challenges. His strength to overcome and give us a path of *hope* makes this book a must read.

—Jeff Dill, Founder and CEO,
Firefighter Behavioral Health Alliance

While I have not experienced anything like what Robert went through, I have seen and helped many horses who have been abused. He can put into words what those horses feel but cannot tell us when they lose their dignity. Their ability to recover, in the right hands, is amazing. It takes compassion without judgment or sympathy to restore self-respect, but it's hard to trust again. Robert's courage to share his process is deeply impactful and empowering, and I love that horses are a part of his journey.

—**Linda Parelli, Founder**
Happy Horse Happy Life

While the details of his trauma are his own, so many parts of what came afterwards are all too familiar for complex trauma survivors, It's all of our stories. *Beneath the Surface* is a raw, authentic testament to the devastation that trauma can bring and the hope, peace, and growth that can accompany healing.

So much of the trauma healing experience is learning to identify the multitude of wounds that have not yet healed. But it's seldom that anyone reaches out and says, "Here's *how* to heal." This narrative does that! Finally, a lesson on *how* to heal. It's more than just a gut-wrenching account of a life mired by trauma, it's a compass that sheds light on a path forward for trauma survivors.

—**Lee Heike, Owner, Hookd Promotions,**
PTSD Survivor, and Equine
Gestalt Coaching Method Client

Beneath
the
Surface

Beneath the Surface

A MEMOIR

ROBERT GOODLAND

The Heart of a Horse
Mondovi, Wisconsin

The Heart of a Horse
Mondovi, Wisconsin
theheartofahorse.com

ISBN (print): 979-8-9913619-0-3
ISBN (electronic): 979-8-9913619-1-0
LCCN: 2024917283

Editing by Melanie Mulhall, Dragonheart, www.TheDragonheart.com
Cover and Interior Design by Journey Bound Publishing

10 9 8 7 6 5 4 3 2 1
First Edition

Contents

Foreword

While at my ranch in Arizona, a friend of mine, Larry, rang my bell to introduce me to a friend of his who was visiting from Wisconsin—a young, handsome cowboy with pain in his eyes. My friend understood I selected applicants for my Gestalt training program and was putting in an excellent word for his young friend, Rob.

The sincerity poured off of Rob as he shook my hand and spoke to me. His eyes darted around a bit, his smile was warm, and I could sense his pain. Based on my first impressions and my friend's praise, I was happy to accept Rob into our program.

Thus began our journey to what has today, after all these years, become a deep and lasting friendship. In our program, each student trains to become a Gestaltist, and part of the training is doing their own exploration of their life. All traumas are examined from the place of how the unfinished business around it affects them in their current life.

Rob did several deep pieces of personal work with me on the unfinished business in his life. He went on to complete our master's program, and today he is one of our top Gestaltists, assisting many others on their own personal exploration. My horses respected and loved Rob, and today his clients meet his own healing herd.

This poignant and tender memoir allows the reader into Rob's heart as he recalls many of the places in his life that were unfinished and held powerful lessons for him as a person. In our community we refer to something called "borrowed benefit," which refers to the experience of often gaining insight into ourselves when we hold witness to another person's deep, vulnerable work. The stories and the lessons in this beautiful book allow the reader borrowed benefit all the way through.

I'm a fortunate two-legged creature who has been able to get to know Rob, and I'm honored to have him use the methodology I have taught him. The profound way in which his clients benefit from his assistance is evident. Now, by reading this book, even more people can benefit from Rob's openness to his lessons learned.

Enjoy the ride,
Melisa Pearce
September 2024

Preface

When I began writing about my life, I wanted to tell my story because I felt it was my only source of significance. I couldn't have been more wrong. I have learned that my life matters because it does. Just like yours.

Through the process of writing about the specific events of my past, I found clarity and peace. Memories that had been repressed surfaced. It has been an incredibly therapeutic endeavor.

But it has been more than that. During the writing process, the reasons for telling my story changed. I no longer wanted to tell the story so that you, the reader, would find significance in my life. I needed to tell the traumatic events, describe my fumbling attempts at relationships, and recount the winding journey I've taken so I could share what I've learned—the beautiful lessons that can only be learned while in the fire—and so sharing would have authenticity to it, would be understood as something more than just platitudes or the regurgitated words of teachers and thought leaders.

My prayer is that someone will read this and find hope that there is a wonderful, passionate, and fulfilling life on the other side of the fire. Life is beautiful. In case no one has told you today, you are enough. Your life matters. The world is a better place because you're in it. You are loved.

By telling *my* story, I pray you realize that *you* have a story within you that someone needs to hear. You are the answer to someone's prayer. Only you can touch their heart. Tell your story.

If, like me, you have struggled with the effects of trauma, felt unease, experienced emptiness within, then I also pray my story and insights can help you on your own healing path toward wholeness. While Pierre Teilhard de Chardin's observation that we are spiritual beings having a human experience has become something of a cliché, it is nevertheless true. After my diving accident, I was given back the gift of time, and I have come to have gratitude for the entirety of my human experience. My hope is that something here will help you on your own journey through human experience and give you assurance that you are not alone.

PART 1: MY STORY

1

How far away can I hide things I don't want to see—or feel? In my basement, in a back room I don't often enter, are boxes I have moved from house to house many times over the years. With each move, I opened them long enough to peer in at the contents. Feelings of overwhelm and hopelessness flooded my body whenever I opened those boxes. I didn't know how to deal with it all. Looking in those boxes is much like looking in on the past traumatic events of my life. How did I make sense of the things that lurked in the shadows? It was easier to simply look the other way and not begin the task of unpacking my past.

Like the boxes in my basement that needed to be dealt with, I would recognize that there were events in my life that needed to be unpacked, and yet I didn't have the tools to unpack and deal with them. It was easier to turn away from the cruel events of my childhood and pretend things were okay. I was who I was because of what others had done to me, and there was no way to change that. I felt damaged and broken, and I believed that was just how my life was going to be. I was dealt a hand that I now had to play. It was out of my control. If memories or feelings arose, I told myself to close the box and put it back on the shelf.

I didn't realize the negative impact that keeping all the bottled up and buried parts of my being was having on my life. Unconscious patterns and habits played out in real time. For many years, I was at the mercy of my past and my emotions tied to it.

Years passed. Slowly, I began to explore and learn. When I felt strong enough to open the barricaded rooms of my history, I took a look at the boxes within them. A feeling of longing swept through me when I looked at the memories of those long-ago events—a longing to change the past. I found myself getting lost in the sadness of what my life could have been if things had been different. Who and what would I have become? What would my life have been like? They were unanswerable questions, and yet I was mired in the past.

The more I explored, the freer I felt to tell my story. I was finding my voice. I was shining a light on the darkness that had surrounded me. The more I told the details of my traumas, the braver I felt. I had significant traumas. Telling the trauma stories made me feel significant, which was something I had never felt. I came to realize that I didn't believe I was significant just because I was alive, I was significant because I had significant traumas. It seemed that was all I had.

Were my traumas really all I had? Had they become my identity? Was the only reason I had a seat at the table because shitty things had happened to me? Who would I be if I let go of the meaning I had created about my life? How could I make peace with my past so I could have peace in my life? What *was* peace? Living in sadness and chaos had become my normal. How could I compassionately untangle the ugliness and find closure, once and for all?

I had been sexually assaulted as a child, and that violation had stolen my childhood. Those events shaped my world for decades, often without my knowledge. Unconsciously, I viewed every subsequent relationship with distrust and skepticism. I had constructed a wall to keep people out except on *my* terms. I had to be in control. I had to keep people from getting too emotionally close to me. I believed that doing so would keep me safe, even though that was a faulty notion and even though it proved wrong again and again.

Instead of providing safety, keeping people at arm's length kept me isolated and alone. I learned the term "lightning strikes" from my mentor, Melisa Pearce. It was an accurate description of that pinpoint moment in time that created a life before and life after the lightning strike— an event that profoundly altered the direction of my life.

It's difficult to say there was a before and after when it comes to my sexual assault. I was eleven years old when it occurred. There wasn't a lot of "childhood" before the events of the summer of 1976, so there really wasn't a "before" to alter. It was just the way life was. I am a childhood sexual assault survivor and I always have been. The trajectory of my life was knocked off course before it really left the launchpad. The mess that the assault created is my metaphorical mess in the basement that I couldn't look at, and as a survival strategy, I simply closed the door.

One of the big unanswerable questions is this: What would my life be like today had Ted Pullman not crossed my path? The fact is that he did. Over the years, the memories of him and how he violated me have gone into a box I've placed high on a shelf. The ugly images were tucked away in the recesses of my mind in a carefully constructed fortress designed to contain the most destructive of events and their ruinous memories.

When the flashbacks of my assault were thrust forward through the cracks and out of the darkness, they came without the socially expected emotions. They arrived without pomp, circumstance, or fanfare. It was as if I were recalling an event that happened to someone else. There was no associated emotion. I was detached. Until my sister-in-law called one day.

"Did you hear the news?" my sister-in-law, Toni, asked over the phone. She still lived in Portage, Wisconsin, the town I moved from in 1979.

I had not heard much news from the town of my birth, and I did my best to avoid gossip. "No," I replied.

Toni explained that a Portage native, Ted Pullman, had been arrested for sexually molesting children. I went numb and felt the color drain from my face. Suddenly I was eleven years old and Ted Pullman was standing before me in the concrete block lifeguard room. I felt nauseous and ashamed.

Two fears quickly entered my mind: Had I told Toni what Ted had done to me all those years ago? Could she somehow sense my shock at hearing her revelation? I felt completely exposed and vulnerable. One touch and my fragile being would crumble to the ground. Suddenly I felt there was nowhere to hide. The world I had crafted that contained the boxed-up memories of my childhood that no one knew about and the world that contained the devastating reality of my assault had just collided.

Why was she telling me this? She had to know! I was terrified. It was as if an earthquake had thrown the box of fragmented memories to the floor, spilling the grotesque images at my feet. Shards of broken glass lay motionless, reflecting an abstract view of my soul and the events from my stolen childhood. I had no choice but to look. What once had no attached emotions instantly had a flood of shame, loneliness, hurt, and betrayal, descending upon me like an inescapable tsunami. Time slowed to a crawl and my head buzzed. What I had once suppressed to the point of viewing it as a blurred image of something that had happened to someone else became sickeningly clear. It had actually happened to me.

In 1976, I was eleven years old. My mother worked in the personnel office at the local hospital. I was in school when she left for work, and she came home a couple of hours after I was home from school. While I don't remember her coming home, I do remember her absence. My childhood memories are only snapshots, mental photographs captured in a moment in time rather than as a movie. Some of those snapshots are of waiting for Mom to come home while watching TV after school. The afternoon TV shows were my babysitters. Waiting for her felt lonely and left an emptiness in the pit of my stomach. For years, hearing the theme songs or seeing an episode of the *Micky Mouse Club*, *Star Trek*, *Gilligan's Island*, or *Hogan's Heroes* would instantly draw forth the painful, empty hole in my gut.

My dog, Ginger, a Shetland Sheepdog, was small enough to sit alongside me in the swivel rocker in front of the TV. My three older siblings, Rita, Kip, and Geoff had moved out of the house years earlier. I was alone with the TV and Ginger. When I was out of school during the summer, I was alone even more. I spent as much time as I could at the beach.

Ted Pullman, a twenty-two-year-old lifeguard at Silver Lake Beach, was a thin man with a kind smile who was popular with many kids at the lake. He offered to help me be a better swimmer and suggested that I come to the lake early in the morning, before the beach opened. I felt seen and included, which was something that was missing for me at home. I felt safe with a man I hardly knew.

The beach was deserted on that cool, overcast morning. There was no reason *not* to trust Ted. It never crossed my eleven-year-old mind that I had been lured to the empty beach for a reason. I didn't see it coming.

I have the luxury of looking back at my abuse through the eyes of an adult. It's easy to judge my eleven-year-old decisions after years of life experience. But to an eleven-year-old with little life experience, Ted was someone who was paying attention to me at a time when it seemed no one else was.

It wasn't out of neglect that I was alone. Mom and Dad had been divorced since I was two, and I wasn't with my dad very often. Mom was distracted with her personal life and working a full-time job. My brother Geoff had been in college for three years. Kip and Rita were a lot older and had families of their own.

During the summer, I left an empty house and I returned to an empty house. I wore a house key around my neck on a dirty white string. I was a latchkey kid. I was an easy mark for a sexual predator like Ted. He was about the same age as my brother Goeff, whom I missed, and I was a lonely kid with no male role model present who craved attention. Maybe I saw Ted as a big brother and mentor that I didn't have and longed for. Maybe at some unconscious level I saw him as a father figure who was offering to help me.

When I'm feeling less than compassionate for my eleven-year-old self, I wonder why I ever said yes to meeting him on that early morning. For years I shamed my inner child for being so gullible and chastised him for not seeing that he was being used. I punished him for not saying no. Someone had to be blamed, and little Robbie took the hit.

I could relate to Christine Blasey Ford, a psychology professor at Palo Alto University and research psychologist at Standford in 2018 when she testified before the Senate Judiciary Committee that a candidate for Associate Justice of the Supreme Court had sexually assaulted her when they were both in high school. She testified that she could not recall some of the details of her assault—something I understood. But some people in support of the appointment said Ford had to be lying. "Who wouldn't remember details like that?" they asked.

Me. That's who couldn't remember details like that. I'm left with only a series of snapshots and brief movie clips of the things Ted did to me over the course of one day. For a long time, I didn't remember going to the lake early in the morning, I just remembered being there and that it was morning. I still don't remember going home. I don't remember struggling with the decision to not tell my mother what had happened or anyone else, for that matter. The lapses in my memory are frustrating. It's difficult to complete a puzzle when you don't have all the pieces. I can't imagine what it would feel like to have someone accuse me of lying because pieces of my memory about the assault are missing.

Many parts are missing, but others are seared into my memory. The abuse began when he removed his swimming trunks while we were in the lake and encouraged me to do the same, which I did. When Ted encouraged me to remove my swimsuit, I felt the water on parts of my body that had been previously covered. Because we were far enough away from shore that I couldn't touch bottom, I hung my swimwear on my arm for fear of dropping it and having it sink to the bottom of the lake. I wondered how I would get home if I lost it. Being naked in public would be humiliating. I was afraid someone would appear on the beach while I was naked in the water. With my trunks on my arm, I could quickly get them back on, and maybe the new arrival would never know I had been without them. The morning air was cool, so the water felt warm.

Ted dove underwater, putting his untanned butt out of the water and gleefully exclaimed, "Great white whale!"

On the sandy beach there was a concrete block building, built years earlier, with three distinct sections. The middle area was for the lifeguards to keep their personal things while they were on duty. It was also where they kept the soda and candy that was for sale. From the outside, there were two windows that beachgoers could walk up to and order their treats. I had never been in that part of the building. I had only looked in from the outside, my eyes barely peering over the wooden ledge when I bought my candy. The lifeguards were respected and that was their room. It was off-limits to anyone else.

On each side of the lifeguard room were the changing rooms. Boys on the left; girls on the right. The concrete floor of the boy's changing room was smooth, cool, and damp on my bare feet, but the room smelled of urine. Kids of all ages used that room, and I was intimidated to be in there alone. I had been bullied in bathrooms at school. Older kids kicked the bathroom stall door open while I was sitting on the toilet, and I was exposed and embarrassed as they stood there pointing and laughing at me. I learned to sit on the toilet and hold my feet against the door so it wouldn't unexpectedly fly open. But I felt safe in the block building with my friend Ted that morning. I wouldn't be bullied.

Ted invited me into the sacred lifeguard room after we swam. I felt special, like I was now an insider. I sat patiently in a chair, my back to the wall while Ted changed out of his wet swimsuit. In the small dimly lit room with the door closed, he stood several feet away from me, facing me. He was naked, and I was aware that his body was more mature than mine. There was a purpose to his actions I didn't understand. He began to masturbate.

At eleven years old, I had no idea what he was doing. I had never seen anything like that before. I was confused and uncomfortable. He didn't finish. I don't recall why he stopped, nor do I have any recollection of why or how that encounter in the room ended.

The next fragmented memory was in the upstairs bedroom of Ted's house. Sunlight poured in through the windows. Ted had me undress and he did the same. He had spring-loaded dart guns, and while we were naked, we ran around the room, shooting darts at each other, ducking for cover, and using the twin bed in the center of the room as protection, trying not to get hit. We laughed as we played, trying not to be hit in the genitals by a speeding dart.

Then we left in Ted's car with the intention of heading back to the beach. We had both dressed to leave the house, but once in the car, he asked me to undress, and he did the same. Driving through town naked, we stopped at the stop sign at the top of the hill on Collipp Street. Ted put the car in park and yelled, "Chinese fire drill!" We jumped out of the car, ran around the car naked, and then got back in and drove off. That intersection was in full view of my dad's house.

As an adult, I'm disgusted by what happened. For years I was ashamed that as a child, I was laughing and having a good time. In an effort to be more compassionate to young Robbie, the question I ask myself now is this: As an adult, if I were looking at an eleven-year-old boy and was hearing the same details of his assault, would I shame that child for laughing and having fun the way I have shamed myself for all these years? Would I shame that child for not telling someone what had happened? For going along with what the abuser had done to that him? Absolutely not! If that young boy questioned why he was laughing and having fun, I would say, "Of course you were laughing. You're a child." I would have far more compassion for that boy than I have, at times, shown myself.

The next memory snapshots are of events that took a dark turn. I was no longer laughing.

Silver Lake Beach was arranged in two sections, the lower section that included the lifeguard building and the beach itself. A steep set of steps cut through a grassy hill and led to the upper section of the park. Up there was playground equipment, charcoal grills, a picnic area, and a large wooden storage building. Inside the old building, picnic tables were stacked for storage. Ted led me inside the building and closed the door. The building was dark except for narrow shafts of sunlight that found their way through the wooden slats of the siding. The concrete floor was cold and damp on my bare feet, just like in the changing room.

Ted positioned himself between me and the closed door. I would have to go through him to escape. I was trapped. He didn't threaten me. He didn't have to. He was an adult, he was bigger than me, and sadly, I wanted his attention—just not like that. I raised my eyes to see the open rafters over my head.

Ted tied a slipknot in one end of a long piece of rope he had with him and threw the other end over one of the exposed roof rafters. The rope slowly swung back and forth as it hung in front of me. "Take off your clothes," he said.

I complied, and he also removed his clothes. He placed the loop of the rope over my testicles and penis and slowly pulled the rope until I was standing on my tiptoes. I was afraid I was going to fall over and wondered what I would do if he pulled so hard that I could no longer touch the ground. I was terrified of what would happen next. There didn't seem to be pain, only fear. Time stood still. As I danced on my toes to keep my balance, I pleaded with him in my mind to let me down. Would he ever let me down?

He eventually let me down, removed the loop from me, and placed it on his testicles and penis. Then he instructed me to do the same thing to him. I did as I was told. I pulled. He danced on his tiptoes. I didn't want to be in that building. I didn't want to do what I was doing. I didn't want to hurt him. For years afterward, I was ashamed that I complied.

I left the building carrying my clothes. Ted made me run down the grassy hill to the lifeguard building naked. I was embarrassed to run naked through the park in full view of any passing cars and in broad daylight.

I have no recollection of getting dressed. No memory of going home. No memory of hiding the truth. I never saw Ted again.

2

The Wisconsin River has its birth in the Lac Vieux Desert, a lake in very northern Wisconsin near the border of the Upper Peninsula of Michigan. It flows south across the glacial plain of central Wisconsin, passing through Wausau, Stevens Point, and Wisconsin Rapids. In southern Wisconsin it encounters the terminal moraine formed during the last ice age and forms the Dells of the Wisconsin River. North of Madison at Portage, the river turns west.

French fur traders crossed over the short stretch of land between the Fox and Wisconsin Rivers, with the earliest recorded travelers being explorers and mapmakers in 1673. A trading post was established on the valuable trade route. That trading post eventually became the town of Portage.

In the late 1960s, Portage was a picturesque small town in rural south-central Wisconsin. The sign at the edge of town on the bridge that crossed the Wisconsin River read "Portage. Population 8000 Friendly People."

If you've ever seen a Norman Rockwell painting, you know the safe, warm, and nostalgic feelings his paintings can evoke. His paintings represent hometowns and everything the word "hometown" represents: Gentle snowfall on quiet city streets and joyful residents bundled up in colorful winter clothing. Parents and children walking hand in hand on the sidewalk in front of quaint downtown shops. Children effortlessly ice-skating on a small frozen pond and a puppy playfully pulling on a child's red scarf. Ice cream at the local soda shop. Small-town baseball games on the Fourth of July.

That was my hometown. When I was a child, it was magical—just like me.

"You know you're a miracle, right?" my mom often said. I always felt special when I heard the miracle story.

"Tell me again, Mommy!"

"Well, you know, I was never supposed to be able to get pregnant," she would say. "And then when I did, the doctor told me, 'Don't get too attached to this baby. You won't carry it to term.' I was giddy with what I knew was coming next. "And when you were born, you were born a month early with nothing wrong with you!" She would always end the story the same way. "See! You're a miracle!"

As a child, I trusted blindly. I trusted my family. I trusted my neighbors. I trusted a lifeguard. It wasn't as if

I were making a choice to trust. I just did. Nothing had happened to make me distrust anyone. Isn't that the way things go? It's good right up until the moment it's not, and you trust right up until the moment someone gives you a reason to not trust.

The adults of Portage didn't lock their doors. As children, we didn't worry about being out at night. When I was growing up, Mom's rule was when the street lights came on, it was time to come home. Often, the fun and games would continue past sunset. We just needed to be closer to home.

My house was in the seven hundred block of Carol Street, which was part of two uninterrupted blocks. I never personally counted, but Mom said there were twenty-two children of varying ages living in my neighborhood. Before the summer I was eleven, I often played with the other kids. I craved connection. Mom wasn't around much and I found the friendships with the neighbor kids, especially the older kids, to be comforting. Most often, I was the one initiating the time together.

Sometimes it might be me and my friend Duffy building a model airplane together in my basement. I would beg Mom to buy me a model just so I could invite Duffy over to build it. He was much better at it than me, and the finished model looked more realistic than it would have if I built it myself.

On another long summer day, there could be a flag football game in the backyard of the next-door neighbors. A few blocks from home, headed toward the Wisconsin

River, was a baseball diamond where we would have baseball games with ten or more neighborhood kids competing for a national championship of our own creation.

My mom had a beautiful old school bell made of polished brass with a mahogany handle that she would stand outside on our front porch and ring when it was time for dinner. I needed to be within earshot so I could hear it and promptly return home to eat.

As the sun set and the streetlights summoned us closer to home, the ravenous horde of infamous Portage mosquitoes the size of small birds descended upon the land. Once we were slathered in bug spray, the evening games close to home might be kick the can or flashlight tag. Any child not coated in mosquito repellant ran the risk of either being covered in red swollen welts or carried away by the beasts.

When the Olympics were on TV, we created our own Olympic-style games, such as who could ride in the clothes dryer the longest. I was a no-show for that event because anything spinning made me sick. Tom took the gold medal for it. I don't believe his mother was so proud of her son's gold medal achievement, and I'm not sure her dryer was ever the same.

Mom, my brother Geoff, and I moved to the small, white Cape Cod home with the bedroom dormers when I was two years old and Geoff was twelve. Mom and Dad had just separated, headed toward their ultimate divorce. My brother Kip, nicknamed after the author Rudyard Kipling, was nineteen years old, and my sister, Rita, was twenty-two when we moved into the Carol Street house. Rita and Kip both lived away from home.

Dad had always been absent much of the time, so living with just Mom didn't seem strange. Mom accused Dad of having affairs with other women. She also claimed that Dad had threatened to kill us, and that was why she finally left him. According to her, he had shown her the pistol he was going to use.

The year before we moved to Carol Street was hard on Mom. Mom carried me on her hip as she went about her daily activities. In time, the constant hip-out posture and the weight of lugging me around caused her back to go out.

Mom was then bedridden and unable to care for me, and because Kip had now graduated high school and was away at college, he was unable to care for me. And Geoff wasn't old enough to care for me. With Mom unable to do any of her normal daily routine, Geoff was left to fend for himself. When Mom was able to get out of bed, my sister would take her to Madison, a thirty-mile trip, for her chiropractic appointments.

I went to a babysitter's home Monday through Friday and sometimes stayed until Saturday. She was an elderly woman with gray hair and handmade dresses. Mom called her Grandma Zimkey, but she wasn't my grandmother. To keep me contained, Grandma Zimkey put me in a playpen set up in her living room in front of the television. Daytime soap operas played continuously.

Grandma Zimkey was afraid of thunderstorms. We would go to the dark basement whenever a storm, big or small, passed through. She had coal delivered through a chute into a small dirty room in the corner of the basement, and that's where we'd go. She wasn't a warm or affectionate woman, but she did her duty.

At times Dad arrived home from the road Friday evening and forgot to pick me up at the sitter. My absence apparently went unnoticed, but when Rita got home from college either Friday evening or Saturday morning and found that Dad had neglected to pick me up, she would get me. I returned to Grandma Zimkey's on Monday morning to start the week again. This routine went on for several months.

A sacred trust had been violated. A truth had been shattered. The one relationship I should have been able to count on without question had been ripped away from me. I could be left with a stranger at any time and not picked up. I could no longer trust that the most important people in my life would be there for me. I could be discarded. I was too young to ask questions and too young to understand what was going on. And yet, it created a scar.

When we moved to the cute white house, I was unable to let Mom out of my sight for a second, even for her to go the bathroom. I sat on the floor under the sink looking up at her as she used the toilet.

For several years, her leaving my sight meant she was never coming back. I was terrified of being alone. Terrified of being abandoned again. As time passed and I got older, I was able to leave the house—and Mom—to go play with the neighbor kids. Mom still asked if it was okay for her to go to the store without me, but eventually, she was able to leave me at home alone.

I learned to accept the emptiness. I could usually cope and manage the hole of loneliness that showed up in my gut. But when I heard the theme song from the daytime soap opera, *As the World Turns*, and saw the sand fall from the hourglass, it was as if each grain of sand had fallen from the hole in my soul. Its absence created a void within me that longed to be filled. *As The World Turns* was the show my babysitter watched religiously, so its theme song was seared into my cells.

After my parents split, my mother referred to my dad as The Great White Father. In all her sweetness, she was very manipulative and could have a very sharp tongue. Spending time at my dad's place created a lot of anxiety for me. Dad didn't operate in the world of feelings. He was not a warm, cuddly man, but he was always kind. I never saw him lose his composure or neutrality. He didn't reveal emotional highs or lows, so he never appeared either happy or sad. He didn't demonstrate or express love to me as his son.

He was a focused businessman. He owned his own businesses, and he was a salesman to his core. Time spent with him at his house on Silver Lake was often a matter of keeping myself occupied while he worked. We did do some fun things together. Occasionally, he took me to a motel in Wisconsin Dells that had an indoor pool. He lived on the lake in Portage, so he wanted me to be able to swim well. The problem was, on our way to do something fun, he usually made one or more stops to make sales calls, which meant I waited in the car for him. The anxiety of being left alone, unsure when he would return, was hard, but I did my best to swallow the rising tide of panic. It seemed it could never be just about us and our time together. I longed to be important to him. I longed to be special.

More than once when I was supposed to spend the night at his house, he ended up bringing me home because I had gotten sick, often vomiting. That usually happened around bedtime. The feelings of homesickness and emptiness would tear at the emptiness in my stomach. On one return trip back to Mom's, I vomited in the bushes as I waited for her to open the front door. Dad didn't hide the fact that he thought I was a mama's boy because I didn't want to stay overnight at his house. I couldn't do it. I didn't know him. I was being separated from my mother and what I believed was the only stable foundation I had.

Inside my young mind, I didn't trust that I would be returned to my mother. He was the one who had taken me to the babysitter's house and left me. And in my young mind, no one came to get me, even though that didn't always happen. If I stayed at his house, how did I know if I could ever go home again? Who could I trust? Who wanted me? Away from the safety of home, the feelings of being discarded and abandoned washed over me like a heavy, dark cloud.

Kindergarten had been fun, a little scary, but overall, a good experience. My teacher was tall. She seemed to tower over me more than the other adults in my life. She was a very kind, compassionate, and patient woman with dark curly hair. It was a toss-up which was better, snack time or story time, where we sat on the floor and Mrs. McElroy was in a chair too short for her long legs and read to us. Snack time was a little tough because it was my first experience with a cardboard milk container that seldom opened the way it was supposed to. At home, Mom made milk in a yellow Sanalac container, mixing the tube of powdered milk in the container. I didn't know what to do with the cardboard milk box.

I made friends and played with small rubber people in a dollhouse, creating families that didn't exist in my world. At nap time, we rolled out our mats and tried to find a comfortable position to eventually sleep for a few minutes. Stories, play, snacks, and naps made kindergarten a pretty comfortable experience.

But first grade was anything but comfortable. I sometimes felt humiliated by my teacher, Ms. Martin, in a way I didn't see her humiliate others. But she didn't stop at humiliation. My babysitter at that time was the daughter of a second-grade teacher, Mrs. Roddick. After school, I went to Mrs. Roddick's room to wait for Sue to get done with school and collect me for the walk home together. Ms. Martin decided that I could not wait for Sue in Mrs. Roddick's classroom and informed me that when school was done, I *had* to leave the building and go home. I was no longer allowed to wait safely for Sue on school property. I didn't feel safe with adults, and I certainly didn't feel safe alone. In my world, I could be left at any moment. Now I learned that I could be kicked out at any moment.

The final straw for my mom was when Ms. Martin announced to her that I was unable to read out loud in class, so there must be something wrong with me. Mom had me read to her all the time at home. The bedtime stories she had once read to me I was now reading to her. Mom knew I could read just fine. She knew the problem wasn't me, it was Ms. Martin. It was clear that I had been bullied into submission, too afraid to allow myself to be seen.

That was it. Mom was done with Ms. Martin. She demanded a face-to-face meeting with her. When the day of the meeting arrived, Mom met me at school at the end of the day. I was in the classroom with them for only a few minutes. The tones were instantly tense, and Mom asked me to leave the room. I was ashamed and embarrassed because I believed I was the cause of their argument.

With my head hung low and my shoulders slumped forward, I retreated down the steps and into the empty hallway. I sat on the floor with my back against the wall-mounted heat register and with my knees pulled to my chest, getting as small as I could. I waited, wishing I could disappear. The volume of their argument rose. Ms. Martin despised me. I could hear it in her voice. The meeting went on for what seemed like forever, and I could not escape. I had no choice but to sit there and listen to them argue about me.

Days later, Mom met with the school principal, requesting that I be moved from Ms. Martin's class. "Mrs. Goodland," he began in his official voice, "if you meet with our school psychologist and she agrees that it's best for Robbie to be moved, I will agree to the transfer." Then he threw in, "We can't have Robbie's mom moving him every time he has a problem with a teacher."

Mom met with the school psychologist. "So, Mrs. Goodland, what teacher's class is it that you would like Robbie removed from?" the psychologist asked in a very pleasant tone, even though she was ready to fight.

"Ms. Martin."

The psychologist raised her hand to stop Mom's next statement. "Say no more. I'll approve the move."

As classes began the next morning, I was instructed to push my desk out of Ms. Martin's classroom. The desk screeched as I pushed it across the tile floor out the door and down the hall to my new classroom at the furthest end. As I entered, they were reading *Fun with Dick and Jane* out loud, and they all turned to look at me. When I was warmly welcomed by the teacher into my new class, it was as if I had been released from a nightmare. Maybe my persecution was over and I could breathe again.

For three years, I didn't feel attacked for speaking or for being alive, but now I was more afraid to speak than I had been before Ms. Martin stripped me of whatever budding self-confidence I'd had. I was afraid I would stumble over words while reading out loud and be publicly ridiculed. I trusted less, feared more, and did my best to be invisible.

In fourth grade I got another lesson in trust. My fourth-grade teacher, Mr. Carter, was a hulking figure of a man with black rimmed glasses and short dark hair. I had no reason to doubt him when he informed us that he had played professional football for the Cincinnati Bengals. He looked like it. He was a very intimidating man.

Early on, it was clear that he liked some students more than others. If a girl in the class had a question and approached his desk, she was instructed to come behind the desk, sit on his lap, and then ask her question. Boys simply stood in front of his desk and asked their questions. It seemed strange to me that he wanted the girls to sit on his lap. I didn't understand why.

I was disciplined once for chasing some girls around the classroom before class started. We were giggling and having fun when Mr. Carter entered the room. We all immediately took our seats, but I was the only boy in the game and the last to find my seat. He promptly called me to his desk at the front of the room. As I stood before him, I noticed that he held four plastic rulers. As the entire class watched, he began to make an example of me. With each word he wanted to emphasize, he rose his voice and slapped the bundle of rulers in his hand in time with his words. The grand finale, the big crescendo of his outburst, was emphasized by striking me and breaking the rulers across my stomach, sending the broken pieces scattering across the floor. Mr. Carter needed to make sure that I fully understood he was in charge. Not that I questioned it at nine years old.

This was not the only time I was the object of his wrath. Following a playground soccer game in which I'd been on the losing team, Mr. Carter made a disparaging comment about my team's loss. Under my breath, I muttered something sarcastic in response, and he heard me. He jerked me by the sleeve of my jacket, pulled me off my feet, and dragged me around the corner of the building and out of the sight of the rest of the class. I was alone with this angry, hulking man, and I could see the rage in his eyes. I was terrified.

He grabbed me by the front of the jacket, raising me to eye level with him. "You will never disrespect me again! Do you understand!" he screamed.

"Yes," I replied through tears. I waited for him to throw me against the brick wall of the building like I had seen happen in the movies and braced for the pain. Instead, he put me down and we walked back to the assembled line of kids in silence. My head hung low, and I felt ashamed as the rest of the kids looked at me in shock. I wanted to hide. I was afraid to be back in the classroom with him again, but I had no choice.

I frequently felt isolated, even from my classmates. I didn't feel like I fit in. Other kids were smarter, could run faster, and were funnier. While other kids grouped together in cliques, I didn't. I was alone in a crowd. I hung out with a couple of friends outside of school, but I frequently felt uncomfortable around their families.

With those in authority at school, I was anything but invisible—even though I often wished I were. But at home, I often felt invisible and excluded.

One of the places I longed to be a part of because it was an integral part of my family was the curling club. The sport of curling was very important to my family. The Goodland name was known not only locally, but nationally because of my dad's and my brother Geoff's success in the sport. Geoff, Kip, and Dad often played together, and they had a bond and a mutual respect I longed to be a part of. But I wasn't quite old enough to play.

Geoff had a natural affinity for the game. Dad mentored him in the fine art of his delivery and the nuances of strategy. If Geoff wasn't in school or with friends, he was on the ice practicing. He was very dedicated, and he was competing and winning everything, even against the adults.

The only time I saw Dad's typically flat affect rouse was in response to Geoff's curling prowess. It was easy to see the pride Dad had in Geoff. I was proud of him too. We all were. But I desperately wanted someone to be proud of me too. And I longed to feel included in the camaraderie I saw between my father and brothers around the sport of curling.

The closest I came to that feeling of inclusion was when Mom and I did things I felt were just between *us*. On several occasions while out running errands with me, Mom saw fire trucks speeding through town with their lights flashing and sirens blaring. "Let's follow them and see where they're going!" she would exclaim with great enthusiasm. And off we'd go in pursuit of the fire trucks. Not only was it exciting, I also felt included during those wild chases.

But at other times, I felt invisible and in the shadow of my family, like an afterthought. In an effort to regain some control, I needed to call attention to myself, so one afternoon before Mom returned home from work, I took several pieces of newspaper and made three separate piles on the floor of our empty one-car garage. With the garage door closed, I lit them all on fire at once. Once they were burning and the flames were reaching higher and higher toward the exposed wooden rafters, I panicked. What had I done! I stomped out the flames with my feet, but the smoke in the garage was so thick, I could barely breathe, so I opened the garage door to let the smoke out.

The remnants of the consumed newspaper, now reduced to ash, littered the floor and swirled in the afternoon breeze. I was frantically trying to sweep them up to remove the evidence when my brother came home. He quickly realized what I had done and told Mom when she returned home from work.

When Mom confronted me, I lied. I told her that I saw a neighbor boy, Tim, running away when I discovered the fires. Soon after, Tim and his mother were standing on the other side of the screen door talking to my mother. Mom summoned me to the door and the truth came out. I was ashamed of what I had done and that I had blamed it on an innocent friend.

I might have learned from incidents like the garage fire, but like many kids, it took more than one misguided act on my part to drive the lesson home. My friend Mark, who lived across the street from me, was a year or so older than me and came from a rough family. Mark would steal Camel cigarettes from his dad and we would go fishing at the river together and smoke. On our way home from school one afternoon, we stopped at the drugstore downtown. Mark wanted me to steal a pack of cigarettes. They were on a rack, not behind the counter like they are today. Mark distracted the clerk, and I nervously put a pack in my backpack. As we attempted to leave the store, the clerk stopped me and asked to see inside my bag. I'd been caught. He asked my name and then took the cigarettes. I was mortified and ashamed. I knew he was going to tell my mom. When I got home, I waited for her to confront me. She never did, and I never shoplifted again.

Fortunately, Mom knew I needed male companionship and mentoring, so she occasionally drove me out to my brother Kip's home in the country after church on Sunday. Kip and his wife, Rose, lived in an old home that was decorated with beautiful antiques. I loved being there with them. Rose was kind and loving, and Kip was a wonderful big brother.

When he was growing up, Kip found his peace by being in nature, usually by himself or with his friend Steve. He loved to hunt and fish, and he wanted that same outlet for me too. He thought it would make me happier. So on my Sunday visits with him, we went hunting. Squirrel hunting with a .22 caliber rifle is a common way kids are introduced to the sport of hunting. During the afternoon, we hunted squirrels, and in the evening, we hunted white-tailed deer with a bow and arrow. He would be up in his tree stand while I sat at its base. He didn't get a deer with that tactic. No surprise there. No deer was going to come near the tree with me sitting under it. And he had to have understood that because he was a lifelong hunter. It was about being at peace in nature. He not only wanted that for himself, he wanted that for me.

The day I killed my first animal broke my heart. Kip and I were hunting gray squirrels on a beautiful fall afternoon. The fallen leaves were dry and crisp, and we sat at the base of a tree, whispering when we needed to talk. All the while, we listened for the rustle of leaves signifying that a squirrel might be rummaging through them, gathering acorns for the upcoming winter. After what seemed like forever, we heard one. As quietly as possible, we moved to get a closer look.

I saw the large gray squirrel climbing up the trunk of a large oak tree. I raised my rifle, and through the open sights of the lever action gun, I saw him hanging on the side of the tree, not moving. I didn't hear the loud, sharp crack of the gun when I pulled the trigger.

I struck him in the back, paralyzing his hind legs. For a moment, he hung there, motionless. Slowly, an inch or so at a time, he began to slide down the tree. With only his front feet to grip the tree, I could hear the sound of his claws scraping against the bark as he desperately tried to cling to the tree, his life slipping away. Eventually, he fell to the ground dead.

I wanted to vomit. I wanted to cry. Tears welled up in my eyes, but I didn't want my brother to see me cry. He was excited that I had succeeded. I was sick. There was nothing exciting about taking the life of that animal. I loved being outside. I felt connected to nature as I listened to the sounds all around me. I loved the bonding time with my brother as he passionately shared with me the love of his sport. But killing the beautiful squirrel was awful.

But with Mom working and only occasional visits to Kip's home, I was becoming accustomed to the solitude. I had toys I played with, often alone with my imagination. Alone to create a world filled with adventures of significance.

I could occupy hours with a courageous G.I. Joe action figure. He was the epitome of the hero soldier, and I pretended to be him—or at least just like him. We zip-lined down the carpeted stairs to get the bad guys on a line of white cotton kitchen string I had taken from Mom's junk drawer. Sometimes we navigated the treacherous terrain of downed Lincoln Logs in his six-wheeled ATV while on our way to save the world. Sometimes we fought off a giant squid in his submarine in the vast and dangerous waters of the Pacific Ocean, also known as the upstairs bathtub.

By the summer of 1976, when I was eleven years old and Mom and I had been alone together for three years, I was alone a lot and often felt insignificant. But summer was a glorious time of year. I was out of school, and I awoke to the sound of mourning doves singing their sorrowful song outside my bedroom window. To me, their song was joyous, not sad. They were singing, "Go Play! Do whatever you want!"

When the morning air was warm and heavy with humidity, I knew it was going to be a great day to go to the beach.

3

Silver Lake Beach was about two miles from my house. To get there, I rode my bike through the quiet residential streets of Portage. Those streets were lined with middle-class homes during a time in our lives when we trusted people. The only time I felt fear while riding to the beach was when I rode through the tunnel under the railroad tracks. At that time, the sidewalk was inside the tunnel with only a rickety wooden railing separating me from the speeding cars passing through the tunnel.

Most of the overhead lights in the tunnel were broken out, making it hard to see. The concrete sidewalk was damp and smelled of urine. Meeting an oncoming bike was frightening because the tunnel didn't feel wide enough for two bikes to safely pass without either hitting handlebars or hitting the tunnel's steel wall and crashing. I did my best to get through it as fast as I could.

Once through the tunnel, I was back in the warm sunshine and fresh air. I pedaled harder up a small hill and past the curling club. A sharp left turn at the Kickapoo gas station and I was almost at the beach.

The bike rack at Silver Lake Beach was just outside the chain-link fence that separated the parking lot from the sandy beach. If the lifeguards were on duty, the gate in the fence was open. If the lifeguards were not on duty yet, the gate was locked and the beach was closed, but it was easy to get around the fence if the gate was locked.

If the gate was locked, I would take off my shoes and socks and tuck my socks deep into my shoes so I didn't lose them. The sidewalk was sandy and easy to navigate, but once I left the sidewalk and stepped onto the sandy beach, it became harder to walk. The loose, warm sand gave way to cool, damp, firm sand the closer I got to the water.

The air was usually warm and the water was cool. After leaving my shoes and towel safely on the beach, I'd walk into the water up to my knees and then dive in headfirst. Completely immersed in the refreshing water, I heard only the muted sounds of water moving around me and my bubbles escaping as I let out a small exhale so water didn't get up my nose. When I reached the surface and took a relaxed deep breath, the air now felt cool and the water felt warm.

I loved being in the water, but I felt most comfortable when I could easily touch bottom. I could swim a little, but

I didn't want to do it for a long distance. I wasn't that good. I knew the older kids had to do a test for a swimming badge that consisted of swimming across Silver Lake. A boat and a lifeguard were alongside them during the quest in case the kid couldn't finish. I knew I couldn't do that. I wanted to be a better swimmer, or at the very least, I wanted to be able to comfortably make it to the high dive.

The high dive was a metal structure with a ladder firmly anchored to the bottom of the lake with huge poles. It was far enough offshore that it was too deep to touch bottom even if you were brave enough to dive headfirst from the tower. It was the older kids who could go out to the high dive, and I wanted to be able to do that.

The lifeguards at Silver Lake Beach sat in their elevated chairs, high above me. They were physically fit and tan, and some of them had white noses from the zinc oxide sunscreen they used to keep from burning. When I looked up at one whoever was on duty, squinting and shielding my eyes from the sun, I saw a kind face that was very focused on the task of saving lives. They were there for us so we could have fun. The sharp shrill sound from the lifeguard's whistle always made me stop and look. Was I doing something I shouldn't?

Everyone had to be out of the water for an hour every day at lunchtime. It was a mandatory rest break. The lifeguards took a break as well. I would dig out my wet, soggy money from a pocket in my swim trunks, and with sand stuck to my wet feet, I stood in line at the concession end of the lifeguard building where the lifeguards were now selling us candy and drinks. The faces that were expressionless and focused moments before were now more animated as they smiled and engaged us. I was just tall enough to see through the open window of the concession stand and make my selection.

One of the lifeguards often behind the counter appeared to be in his early twenties. He was a thin man with a kind smile. Children seemed to gravitate toward him more than the other lifeguards, and I often saw several kids around him when he wasn't on duty in his lifeguard chair. He was playful with them and there was always laughter in his presence.

In time, I was included in the fun, and I looked forward to seeing him when I went to the beach. Sometimes I saw him teaching other kids to swim. Eventually I learned his name was Ted Pullman.

He took an interest in me, asking about my family and what I liked to do. I felt included when he asked me to join the group of children in his sphere. I felt special and my heart swelled with affirmation when I was singled out for attention.

I told him about my family: How my parents were divorced and that all of my siblings were now gone. I told him that my mom worked at the hospital all day and that I wore a key around my neck so I could get into my house. When I told him of my desire to learn to swim better so I could go to the high dive, he offered to help. He said that he would have the most time for me if we could meet early in the morning, before the beach opened. I jumped at the chance. I was excited to have a big brother again.

So on a cool overcast morning, I parked my bike in the bike rack at the fence separating the parking lot from the beach. My bike was the only bike in the rack. There was only one car in the parking lot. The gate was locked. The beach was closed. I took off my shoes and socks and tucked my socks deep into my shoes. I walked around the fence and unknowingly into the end of my innocence. Ted Pullman was waiting for me.

4

I'm not sure if he lied to do it, but Dad got me onto the curling club ice to begin teaching me to curl in the fall of 1976 when I was eleven instead of the required twelve years old. Maybe it was lie of omission. No one asked; we didn't tell. I had watched Geoff and my family curl for years, so I was well versed in the sport. Now it was my chance to learn, be a part of my family, and have Dad be proud of me.

It was clear from the beginning that I didn't have the same natural talent my brother had. Added to that, I had little focus and I was always emotional. I cried a lot. I felt more isolated and alone than I had ever felt before. I was an outsider. I felt I didn't fit into any group, let alone the group that my family was so intrenched in: the world of competitive curling—the world I had so desperately wanted to be a part of only a short time before.

Being the unemotional person he was, Dad had no idea what to do with me when I became emotional, usually sobbing. From his position, there was no apparent reason for it. He had no idea what had happened to me that summer.

No one knew what Ted had done to me because I hadn't told anyone. Even though I had no frame of reference for what had happened, I knew it was wrong. I was ashamed for having felt special when he invited me into the lifeguard room and for laughing when we ran around his bedroom naked, shooting darts at each other. Even my young, naïve mind sensed the twisted nature of it, but I was too immature to understand that I'd been taken advantage of and violated by a person of trust. So I felt ashamed and guilty. And when the memory of the sick, terrifying activity in the storage room came flooding back, the horror of it didn't just fill me with shame, it left me wanting to compartmentalize it in some deep corner of my mind where I could keep it hidden. But it couldn't be consistently and completely suppressed, which left me grappling with emotional meltdowns I didn't even understand myself.

Fortunately, curling put me in the path of other kids, many of them older than me. And through those kids, I found the one thing that made the shame and emptiness fade away. For once I felt as though I fit in. But through the older boys at the curling club, I found drugs.

I was twelve years old the first time they invited me to smoke pot with them. Being included in their group—any group, for that matter—felt good. They were older and were fun to be around. It appeared they wanted me to be with them. I loved the feeling of being removed from reality when I was stoned. Being high was an escape. It was a way of leaving the chaos and sadness of my life while being in the world in an entirely new way. The world I suffered in was gone when I was high.

Wausau First Chance Bonspiel was the first curling event of each season. Hence the name. It was the first chance of the year for teams to get out and play together. Dad and I went every year, and sometimes Geoff and Kip came along. We usually won.

I was trying desperately to fit in, and at thirteen, I was introduced to the magic of alcohol. Curling always had a rich social tradition. When I say social, I mean drinking. At the competitive level, the sport was very serious. At the local level and at bonspiels, as the tournaments were called, drinking was engrained in the social fabric of the event. Tradition dictated that when two teams finished their game, the winning team bought the first round for the losing team. Both teams sat together and socialized as a show of good sportsmanship.

The night I was introduced to alcohol, a girlfriend of one of my brother's friends was paying attention to me and being nice to me. I felt included and it felt wonderful. I was a novelty in the room because there were no other thirteen-year-olds playing on a men's team, and I was feeling like a big shot. I was sitting on her lap, and she began offering me sips of her drink, vodka and orange juice. I took them, and I began going to the bar to get her more when her glass was empty. I'm sure it was cute to have the young kid delivering beverages to her. Each time, on my way back to the table, I consumed part of her drink. Pretty soon I was delivering rounds for others at the table, and I drank some each time. When I began to feel the tell-tale signs of being drunk, I saw it as fun. I was less inhibited and part of the group. My troubles were gone, as was my social awkwardness. I loved it.

Dad was at the table with me and saw me drinking. Neither he nor anyone else discouraged it. Maybe I was invisible. By the end of the of the evening, I had made a comment that was very derogatory to my dad in an effort to be seen as part of the group. Even through the effects of the alcohol, I felt shame for what I'd said. By the time we returned to the motel room, I was drunk and Dad knew it. Still nothing was said.

From that point on, if I could get my hands on alcohol or pot, I would. I began stealing alcohol that Mom had tucked away for the rare times she had people over. She didn't drink at all, so I knew she would never notice if some was missing.

If alcohol was present, I did my best to be involved. I was a sad drunk, not a happy one. What once made me feel less inhibited and free had quickly turned on me. When I was drunk or high, sadness replaced freedom. It was still an escape, but the place it took me to was dark. Alcohol allowed me to feel less. The sharp peaks of my pain, shame, humiliation, and loneliness were flattened. Not gone but muted. Alcohol and drugs were making my life tolerable, not better. Profound sadness became normal.

Mom was more and more distracted. Less present. Less connected to me. The old familiar feelings of abandonment were flooding through the cracks. My use of drugs and alcohol couldn't save me from the onslaught of loneliness any longer.

One night, after a particularly bad fight with Mom, a family friend, Bill Armson, showed up in my room to straighten it out and make me see the error of my ways. I was sitting in bed with my knees pulled tight to my chest when he came into my room, there to save the day. He did his best to impress upon me what a horrible son I was being to my mother, and he demanded that I treat my mother with more respect. I wondered why my mom had called him to intervene.

The summer I was fourteen, Mom was making plans for us to move. I was at a point where death seemed like a better option than moving. I had nowhere to run. I did my best to mentally prepare for the move, but I had no idea *why* we were moving. I was trying desperately to hold on to what I knew. The last vestiges of me were being devoured by a darkness that was descending on me, and a part of me was excited to move because I thought I could escape the ever-present despair if we moved. And yet, this was my home and it was all I knew.

I was uncomfortable everywhere, and I began to realize why. I couldn't escape myself. I came with me wherever I went. It was as if there was a never-ending scream stuck deep inside me. I was being devoured from the inside out. I didn't want to die, and yet I felt backed into a corner. The shadows were calling for me and I could feel a sense of resignation settling in. I frantically searched for a safe place to fall apart, and while I desperately wanted Mom to see me, she was emotionally somewhere else.

My final summer in Portage was filled with arguments with my family. I felt I was failing everywhere and letting everyone down. I was told I wasn't doing enough to help with the move, and my brother Geoff was angry about that. Not only was there sorting and packing to be done, we also needed to make repairs to the house so it was appealing to a potential buyer.

A few houses past the beach lived a kind woman, Sandra, who taught at the elementary school. I never had her as my teacher, so I hadn't met her at school. Like Ted Pullman, several other kids I knew were drawn to her and spent time with her at her beach house. She felt like a safe person to be around. She had a long pier, and we sat at the end of it for hours, feet dangling in the cool water, talking about life—my life.

She was easy to talk to and she cared. Even though I felt I could trust her, I never told her about Ted and what he had done to me. I didn't intentionally withhold that. I had locked those events far away in my mind. They were stashed so far away that even I couldn't touch them. Some part of me seemed to know that to do so would be catastrophic.

I had no idea how to ask for help. By then, just weeks before the move, I no longer wanted to exist. Being alive was painful, but the thought of dying was scary. I was stuck. I couldn't leave the world, but the prospect of living was crushing. I didn't know how to stay and I couldn't scream. Early one summer morning before Sandra was awake, I sat at the end of her pier with a very large knife I'd brought from home. I begged and bargained with myself to find the courage to finally end the pain by ending my life.

Sandra saw me sitting alone on her pier, came out, and sat with me in my despair. She took the knife away from me and brought me into her house, where she held me while I cried.

I held on as we prepared our home for sale. It didn't take long for the house to sell. We were moving to Eau Claire, a distance of nearly a hundred and fifty miles from Portage, and the first trip to Eau Claire was filled with stress and anger. Once again, Mom and my brother were angry with me because I hadn't done my share to help with the move. Geoff and his girlfriend, Mary, had done more than their share of the work for Mom and me. We made two trips between Portage and Eau Claire that day. Mary and Geoff were exhausted and I was lost. Before the final trip of the move, I said goodbye to my friends.

We moved into an old white duplex near the Eau Claire branch of the University of Wisconsin. Geoff had convinced Mom that she should purchase a student rental to help defray her expenses because she was now unemployed, but the house needed a lot of cosmetic work. As a college student rental, the house had been allowed to slip into disrepair with peeling wallpaper, chipped paint, and unfashionable muted colors. The summer before ninth grade was spent peeling old paint and layers of wallpaper off the walls with a wood chisel. It was a unique type of pain to have seven layers of paint and wallpaper get jammed under a fingernail like a medieval torture technique as I pushed the wood chisel across the plaster wall.

I was doing what was expected of me. I didn't want to disappoint anyone. I didn't want to be chastised again for not doing my part.

5

I didn't know a soul at my new school. There wasn't one familiar face to gravitate to, no safe place to land. I'd felt like an outsider for years, even when I knew people and they knew me. Here, in an old redbrick building that was due to be vacated the following year, I had not even a single ally. I felt alone like never before.

A pretty, blonde girl stopped at my locker while I was crouched down getting my books out. For a brief moment, I felt seen, but I was only capable of showing anyone the outward mask I wanted them to see. I didn't feel safe enough to share the truth about the growing demon that was tearing at me from the inside out.

"Hi! Are you new here?" she asked.

"I am," I said timidly.

She flashed me a smile. "My name is Judy. Judy Green."

Judy had a bubbly personality, and I would find that she was a popular girl within her clique. She might not have been a leader within her group, but she certainly was Miss Congeniality. She was the first person at Central Junior High School who invited me in. I enjoyed her company and friendship. She was the first person I could trust in my new world. Her smile and cheerful hello were an oasis in a desert of uncertainty.

Judy smoked pot, and I fit right in with her and her friends. We got stoned before school, during school, and after school. Frequently, we got high walking home from school, and I reeked of pot and cigarette smoke when I met my brother Geoff at my house to begin the afternoon of remodeling projects. I was always paranoid of being found out, and I had to focus on the work at hand. While high, it was an exercise in extreme concentration to walk in the attic. It had no floor, so I had to focus to be sure I stepped on the floor joist to avoid falling between the joists and through the ceiling to the room below.

I was trying desperately to fit in and have a group I was a part of. I tried football. The coach was a short, round man with a huge voice he was not afraid to use. He yelled when I did something well and he yelled louder when I didn't. The other kids on the team had been playing football together for years by the time I joined the team, so I was something of an outsider. That was compounded by the fact that I didn't really know what I was doing when I was on the field. My being an outsider on the football team was an outward representation of how I felt inside everywhere in my life. I didn't fit in. I didn't belong. I wasn't supposed to be here.

I had never done anything that required me to push through physical pain like playing high school football did. The rest of my life required similar effort. I was shrinking, getting ever smaller, rather than rising up to meet life head-on. It was becoming more and more evident that I didn't have the resiliency to cope with the physiological demands of anything that resembled a challenge. I didn't have it in me. I was exhausted and defeated. My depression and drug use were pulling me in one direction and my attempt to do something healthy like playing an organized sport was pulling in the other. I was losing my grip on the light, losing the battle. I quit football before the first season was over. On top of all the other dark feelings I was experiencing, I could now add the shame and embarrassment of being a quitter to the growing list of failures.

When I was drunk, suicide felt closer. Like a shadow that was not my friend, incessantly calling to me, its voice was much more seductive and alluring when I was lost in the fog of my growing addiction. I walked the halls of the junior high school with small visible slashes on my wrists and arms from self-harm, and I was toying with the idea of *really* cutting them. I was afraid to live and afraid to die. Embarrassed to be such an emotional mess, I wanted to hide from the world. At the same time, I desperately wanted someone to notice my arms, to notice me. I wanted to be seen. In a sea of people, I felt invisible.

Through Judy, I began to find kids to hang with, even though they were the ones using drugs and drinking. On occasion, I found myself with the jocks, the stars of the football and basketball teams. They definitely weren't my tribe, but I discovered that even they were drinking, smoking, and doing drugs like the burnouts who were my friends.

One night, while I was riding in the car and drinking with them, one of them stole a case of beer from Johnny's gas station. It was a reminder that people weren't always who they presented themselves to be. Everyone wore masks, and sometimes what lurked behind them was dangerous. Ted Pullman had taught me that, and the jocks reminded me that I couldn't trust people and who they said they were because people lied.

Some of my friends who were jocks were having sex, and they bragged about it. I had not had sex yet and I was envious of them. Sometimes I even waited outside someone's home while they had sex. They were not only accepted by society because they were athletes, they were also accepted by girls. And the girls were willing to have sex with them. I wondered what it was like to be *that* accepted.

One evening a female classmate wanted to have sex with me. Not only did we have sex, we did it in her home, upstairs in her room, with her parents downstairs. It was my first time and it was everything you would think it was: awkward and clumsy. We were on her carpeted floor, so it was also very uncomfortable. I walked the three blocks home feeling different inside, like I had accomplished something, but I didn't feel good about myself, and I certainly didn't feel any more complete.

I was looking for external validation to an internal issue. It didn't work. For a short moment, I felt okay. I felt accepted. It didn't last long.

My world had taken another big shift that night and no one noticed. I had participated in a rite of passage for a teenage boy. My sex talk with my dad didn't happen until well after the fact. It was a short and crude two sentences that constituted a set of orders: Don't fuck anything you wouldn't eat first. And know that they can get pregnant at any time.

I thought to myself, good talk.

There was no doubt in my mind that Mom loved me, but she was distracted. She appeared as lost as I felt. I didn't understand why, but I felt the distance between us. She was going through the motions, doing her best to fulfill her obligations. Dinners had deteriorated from home-cooked meals to microwaved TV meals. Sometimes she didn't even want to put in *that* much effort. Some evenings we drove to Dairy Queen and had Peanut Buster Parfaits for dinner.

We were fighting more and more about what felt like everything. We fought about the length of my hair. We fought about my curfew, which I was ignoring on a regular basis. We fought about my allowance and whether or not I even deserved an allowance. We fought over my failing grades. It's hard to say what came first, her pulling away, which led to the fighting, or the fighting, which led to her pulling away. Or perhaps they were unrelated. Whatever the scenario, both were happening. And I felt increasingly unsettled, unsafe, and isolated.

I didn't have a driver license yet, so my ten-speed bike or my skateboard were my forms of transportation. I discovered that I could ride my bike when I was drunk, plus I had the misguided belief that the trip home in the open air would allow me to sober up and air out. Maybe the smell of alcohol, cigarettes, and pot would magically blow away as I pedaled my way home from whatever party I had attended.

Sometimes I found myself miles from home, far outside the city limits, at an impromptu party near Otter Creek. The creek was a small, well hidden, and popular swimming hole. When an older kid showed up with beer or pot, they always seemed willing to share.

It was there, after a night of drinking by the creek and off in the shadows, that I had sex for the second time. A very pretty and popular girl wanted to have sex with me, and she was among the students I felt were better than me. I figured that being accepted by her in that way must mean that I was okay. And being seen and accepted by any female felt good.

Afterward, I again felt empty. I didn't feel loved or even satisfied. It felt cheap and I felt used. It was fun because she was a beautiful girl, and there was a certain sense of hollow significance because she was willing to be that intimate with me. But once again, it was a desperate grasp at belonging that only lasted a few minutes.

My emptiness wasn't because the sex was *bad* or anything like that. It was me. It was the reason I was there. It was the reason I was desperately seeking connection and desperately wanting to feel accepted for who I was. But it was more than that even. I wanted to feel that I was enough, and I wanted to be accepted just for being alive. I was doing everything I could to fill an emptiness within me that couldn't be filled by an external source. I felt emptier than before. Sex didn't fill the ever-present void within me.

After the renovation work was completed on the student rental Mom and I lived in, Mom was completely done with living above a rowdy group of male college students. She purchased a ranch style house in a quiet neighborhood. All three of the bedrooms were small, and I wanted more privacy. But there was another room in the finished basement, and that was to be my room. It was larger than the upstairs bedroom and away from prying eyes. I played my records so loud, they rattled the dishes in the kitchen sink at the other end of the house. Mom hated it. I sang at the top of my lungs to my favorite songs by Foreigner, Rush, and April Wine. Pat Benatar's songs spoke to my aching heart. "Hell Is for Children" reverberated through me like an anthem.

Mom was slipping further into her depression. We were both drowning.

The life I knew was in Portage. I was torn between the heartache my hometown represented and the fact that it also represented the only sense of connection I'd had. I wanted to see the friends I'd left behind, and I could stay at my dad's place, even though I knew we wouldn't spend much time together. It was easier for Mom to put me on a Greyhound bus than drive me to Portage, so I went by bus. Mom had escaped Portage and had no interest in returning.

Sandra was one of the people I appreciated reconnecting with. She was a female figure in my life who paid attention to me, and I liked the attention. I felt special, like I mattered. To her, my pain mattered. She listened.

During one of the visits to Portage that our friendship became cumbersome and awkward. I was fifteen years old when our relationship turned sexual one afternoon at her house. Like my other sexual encounters, I didn't feel good about myself when it was over. The attention was nice, but it felt awkward and cheap.

I couldn't talk about my sexual experience with Sandra. I was underage and she was a teacher. She would likely be fired from her teaching job and even arrested because of it. I needed to keep it hidden. It was the only time we had sex, though we continued to be friends.

But sex had now become a way for me to prove to myself that I had value.

6

"Why the *fuck* is *he* here!" I screamed at my mother. "Because I love him."

My relationship with my mother had been growing more argumentative by the day. I wanted her to throw me out. It would prove to me that I was as unworthy as I felt.

Feeling my mother pull away from me little by little over the years was like a slow, painful death. Now that *he* was in her life, it seemed proof that I had no place in her world. I had been replaced by someone I had only met a couple of times in my life, and whenever he was spoken of prior to this invasion, he was always referred to as "a family friend." I wanted the bullet to the head. At the very least, I wanted to be thrown out so I could be released from what I saw as a prison.

Bill Armson arrived at our new house on Mitscher Avenue in Eau Claire like Darth Vader coming to crush the rebellion once and for all. He had just left his wife, the mother of his five adult boys, and immediately moved into our house.

He arrived with an iron fist, laying down all the rules, laws, and mandates that, in his opinion, Mom had clearly not laid down. He believed she'd failed to provide enough strict parenting and saw that as the cause of my ongoing rebellion.

I found my voice. Through tears of hurt, betrayal, and abandonment, I screamed at my mother, begging her to make him leave.

"I would rather cut off my right arm than lose Bill!" she replied.

There it was. Nowhere in there was anything about feeling me slipping away, of feeling she was losing me as her son and not wanting that to happen. There was no sense of caring for me in what she said, let alone any statement about my importance in her life. There was nothing about choosing me over him, which was what I desperately wanted. I felt unwanted and unwelcomed. My acceptance in that home was clearly conditional. If I behaved according to their definition of good, I was wanted. If I struggled or challenged anything, I needed to be punished. If I begged to be seen, heard, and understood, I needed to be crushed and taught to respect. Mom's words to me were that I could do anything, even commit murder, and she would still love me. But her actions were saying something completely different. I was now in the way of Mom's new life. She wasn't willing to lose Bill, but she was willing to lose me.

After Bill moved in, Dad quit paying child support for me. I was in need of a new pair of shoes, and Mom said she couldn't afford them. So when I was about to take a bus to Portage to visit Dad and some friends, she said I should tell Dad I needed new shoes, and since he wasn't paying support, he should buy them for me. I did just that. Instead of buying me new shoes, he went to the basement and found a sample pair of shoes that fit me from one of his vendors. They were ugly and uncomfortable. I found myself in the middle of an argument between Mom and Dad, and I felt like a pawn.

On a bitterly cold February night, I met friends at the local bowling alley. With nothing but the clothes on my back, I ran away from home with a girl I barely knew. She had run before, so I figured she knew what she was doing. I had no idea what *I* was doing. When my curfew passed, I knew I had crossed a line at home. I was now committed to my decision to run. There was no turning back.

For the first time, I felt in control of my destiny. I was no longer at the mercy of those around me. I felt both empowered and afraid. I also felt guilty for what I knew I was doing to my mother.

The temperature that night sank to ten below zero, and the cold night air ripped through my clothing. In the early morning hours, Suzie found a house where we could stay. A man answered the door when she knocked, and they chatted for a moment. He stepped aside and let her in, but as I stepped toward the open door, he looked me in the eye and closed the door in my face.

Without realizing what I had done, I had again placed my fate in the hands of someone else. I had wrongly felt that Suzie and I were partners in running, but I quickly learned that I was excess baggage in yet another person's life. I felt discarded and abandoned.

I knew I would die if I slept outside, but I couldn't go home. I found an open basement door in the back of the house. Warm air rose up through the stairwell, and I curled up as tightly as I could on the dirty wooden steps, thinking I'd be able to stay warm enough and would hear footsteps above in the morning. I didn't want to be alone. I wanted to be reunited with the girl I believed was my friend.

Everywhere I looked in my life I only saw that I could be left, that I was not worth keeping around. That I was an inconvenience. Lives were better off without me. I believed that my life held no value to anyone.

The cold continued to seep further into my bones, and I couldn't stop shivering. I couldn't stay on those steps, so I left the basement, walked through a small park in the middle of town, and found that the door to the YMCA was open. In the entryway was a radiator that was invitingly warm, so I sat with my back to it and slept.

When I awoke, the sun was starting to come up. I walked back to the house to see if anyone was awake yet and peered through a window to see only darkness. On my way back to the YMCA and its warm radiator, an Eau Claire police cruiser passed by as I walked through the park. He had apparently seen me because he turned his car around, and with nowhere to hide, I ran.

I ran as fast as I could toward the river, darting between cars in a parking lot and hoping he would lose sight of me. He didn't. As I ran on the river bank along a tree line behind the YMCA, I could hear his pounding footsteps getting closer. When I went over the top of a small snow bank, I stopped and flattened myself on the ground thinking he would run over the top of me. Then I could jump up and run in the opposite direction. As I lay there terrified, he ran over the top of me and then stopped. Turning and facing me, he said, "Hi Robbie."

I was caught.

For the first time in my life, I was placed in the back of a police car. "My name is Officer Steve Page," he said. "If you'd continued to run, I would have caught you because I was a high school long-distance track star."

We both chuckled a little.

"Your mom is worried sick about you. Why did you run away?"

I told him about the problems I was having at home and about Bill, a man I didn't really know, moving in. I begged him not to take me home. As he began to drive, he said he wasn't going to take me home. We were just going to drive and talk a little. But the entire time we talked, he was driving me back home. I wanted to die. There was little conversation when we arrived at the house. I went downstairs to my room and went to sleep while Officer Page talked to Mom and Bill.

Mom, Bill, my brother Geoff, Goeff's wife, Mary, and a friend of my mom had plans to go cross-country skiing that day, and despite my protests, it was decided that I would be joining them. I spent the afternoon doing something I had never done and didn't want to do, but I felt shame and embarrassment for what I had done to my mother, so I did my best to put on the mask that everything was okay. I was far from okay.

When we returned to Mom's house, Geoff and Mary had a conversation with Mom and Bill about what to do with me.

"I want Robbie to come live with us for a while," Geoff said.

"Absolutely not!" Bill replied. "I want him to get up every morning from this day forward, look at me across this table, and know that what he did was wrong!"

Geoff had only been married for two years when he and Mary fought Bill to take me into their home. Taking on a teenage delinquent who was defiant and abusing drugs and alcohol was no easy thing to do, and they didn't have to do it. But they wanted to. They wanted to protect me, and it was clear to my brother that staying with Mom and Bill was not going to be the best thing for me. I left the home my mother shared with Bill and moved into my brother's house—a far more stable and healthy place to be than with my mom and stepfather, even though Geoff was only ten years older than me.

To get me under control at school, Geoff and Mary established a postcard system. I hated it because it held me accountable. They met with each of my teachers, and at the close of each meeting, they left a handful of self-addressed, stamped postcards to send back to them.

When I missed an assignment or got behind in class in any way, my teacher jotted a quick note to my brother and dropped it in the mail. I didn't realize the postcards were coming, but when they arrived at the house, Geoff and Mary were on me instantly to get my homework done. It was a very effective system that got my grades headed in the right direction, despite my kicking and screaming.

Two school subjects that kept me from dropping out of high school were band and drama. I played trumpet from sixth grade through high school, and I was always in the first section and usually toward the top. Pep band was my favorite. There we got to play the popular songs of the day, dress up in costumes, and cheer on our sports teams. Creating music allowed me to focus on something other than my problems, and I loved being a part of something bigger than me.

Tom Atkinson was also a trumpet player, and he sat near me. We were often testing for the same chair in band. We swapped seats on occasion because sometimes he did better than me and sometimes I did better than him. He was a nice kid who liked to joke around and have fun.

My English class was right after lunch. I sat in the front row, right in front of Mr. Simonson, and Tom sat directly behind me. With that class being right after lunch, I was usually high. For some inexplicable reason, Tom lit the back of my hair on fire one day. I heard his lighter click twice and then heard the sizzle of my hair burning! I jumped, putting the flames out with my hand. The ensuing smoke hit Mr. Simonson directly in the face.

Not long after that, Tom was diagnosed with a brain tumor and died the following year. It was another difficult loss for me, along with the death of another friend, a girl I knew from drama class. His death was further proof that nothing in my life was permanent.

Despite band and drama, I was spiraling out of control. The summer after my sophomore year, Sandra paid for me to go to a Christian summer camp in Saranac, New York, called Young Life. There I met other kids who were struggling like me—the misfits and outcasts—and we seemed to gravitate to one another. There was lots of prayer, along with outdoor activities. I went parasailing for the first time and we hiked the nearby hills. The scenery was magnificent. I learned to tie a bandana several different ways to wear as a hat, a skill I found to be very useful.

The purpose of the trip was to save me from myself and maybe save my soul. I wasn't saved. I felt unworthy of being saved. I did my best to go through the motions, but inside I felt disconnected, not only from the the other kids and the world at large, but also from God. I cried a lot. The hole in my being was growing larger.

I was home from New York for only about a week before I was off again. My brother Kip, who lived in Juneau, Alaska, had offered to have me stay with him for the rest of the summer. I have no doubt the offer was intended to accomplish several things: help me, guide me, maybe give me a sense of direction, and give Geoff and Mary a much-needed break from the chaos I was creating in their life together.

I had never flown on a plane by myself prior to that trip and had to change planes in Seattle, Washington. My brother's girlfriend, Robin, picked me up at the airport in Juneau, and it didn't take me long to learn that she liked to smoke pot. I used that knowledge as permission and a foothold. It seemed rather hypocritical to tell me I shouldn't smoke pot when she was.

I got a job working as a busboy in the restaurant at the Baranof Hotel in downtown Juneau. I'm sure Kip wanted me to have the job to provide structure, but what it did was give me spending money for pot and quarters for the video games at the arcade at a local hangout called PJ's. I found friends there who enjoyed the same things I did.

My shift at the Baranof started early in the morning. My ride picked me up as the sun was barely breaking, and I finished work before Kip, which meant I returned from work to an empty house. I entertained myself by playing records, and after Kip was done with work at IBM, we often went fishing. Kip owned a large boat, and we cruised the inland waters around Juneau, fishing for halibut and salmon. He also began teaching me to drive his stick shift pickup truck on the roads that snaked their way through the twisting and turning gravel mountain roads outside Juneau.

Mostly, though, I wanted to spend my free time drinking and doing drugs with the kids I saw as friends. Because of that, my time with my brother was a gift I wasted. He had offered me a chance to see beautiful country I had never seen before and would never have had a chance to see at that point in my life had he not offered to have me stay with him that summer. He offered me the gifts of his time, attention, guidance, and wisdom. The very thing I was frantically searching for, love and acceptance from my family, was presented to me on a silver platter, and I turned my back on it.

By the time I returned to Geoff's house when the summer was over, I had begun to feel a stirring within me that something needed to change. It was becoming clear that my addictive behavior was going to kill me if I didn't take my own life first. I stopped smoking pot but kept drinking. Unfortunately, I became intensely depressed when I was drunk and wanted to die. One night, I walked on the very edge of a busy highway, praying that a car would jump the curb and hit me. I didn't have the courage to step into traffic.

Mom and Bill were married during my junior year in high school. I couldn't be happy for their union, and my smile was fake. He was staying. My mother had chosen Bill over me. I could never go home.

Shortly after they were married, they put down our family dog, Ginger. I'd grown up with her, and she'd been my faithful companion. Mom didn't tell me when Ginger became sick or that they had to put her down. She was gone and buried in the backyard before I was told what had happened, and I was devastated. I felt betrayed by Mom. And I hadn't even had a chance to say goodbye.

That same year, my first friend in Eau Claire, Judy Green, died. She'd been a passenger in her boyfriend's car when he was pulled over by the police. As her boyfriend sat in the back of the squad car, Judy stood outside the officer's window, talking to him. A passing car, driven by another classmate, hit and killed her.

I attended her funeral and her burial. It was a devastating loss. The way she died was the way I had prayed not so long before that to be taken—hit by a car on the highway. She'd been taken instead of me. I missed my friend when she was gone. I'd never told her how much it meant to me that she'd said hello when I was new to town, that she'd seen me and recognized I was new and alone. I'd never told her how special she was.

I was hurting, and I sought comfort and validation from anywhere I could find it. A married woman named Lori who was friends with a classmate of mine had seen me in a school play and took an interest in me. When Lori wanted to have sex with me, I didn't say no.

It was a complicated affair because we were always dodging her husband. He was a large man, muscular and angry. During the course of my relationship with his wife, I spent time with them together, and it was awkward. We played guitar together. We drank together. Occasionally, Lori picked me up from school at lunchtime and took me back to her place, where we ate lunch and had sex. She delivered me back to school in time for class.

One afternoon, her husband unexpectedly came home, and I had to jump out of her bedroom window and run through the woods to avoid getting caught. Another time I hid in a bedroom closet until he left again. My life and my decisions were completely out of control. I was drinking more and more, and the bottom was falling out of my life. I was either creating situations that I needed to hide from others or I was actually hiding. Either way, my life was one secret after another.

Then I made a decision following a very strange night. I was ten miles north of Eau Claire, trying to see a girl I was interested in. Her dad caught me sniffing around the house, and he was pissed. He didn't want the likes of me anywhere near his daughter and said so in no uncertain terms. Somehow, he knew or suspected I had a problem with drugs and alcohol, and he happened to be a counselor at the drug treatment center in that town. He got in my face and yelled at me that I needed help. His words resonated with me. He was right.

I hitchhiked back to my brother's house. The man who picked me up had to move the twelve-pack of beer off the front seat so I could sit down. Clearly, it was a sign. That night I made a decision that would change my life: I decided to go to an alcohol rehab center.

When I told Mom I wanted to go to treatment, she refused. "There is no reason for you to go!"

"I need help," I said. "I've tried to quit on my own. Something's wrong. I can't live like this anymore. I feel like I want to die."

"I'm not paying for that! Insurance won't pay for that!"

"Whatever insurance doesn't pay, I'll pay," I replied.

Mom didn't understand the gravity of my situation. She wasn't living in my skin. She didn't know how bad it was for me. She didn't know how many times I had thought about taking my own life, nor did she want to know. She didn't know that I had walked inches from oncoming traffic, begging through tears for a car to hit me. She didn't know I'd sat with a razor blade against my wrist, deeply searching for the courage to cut myself. How could she have known? She wasn't looking and I didn't tell her.

7

They took everything during my check-in. Once I'd promised Mom I'd pay for whatever insurance didn't pick up, she relented and checked me into a drug and alcohol treatment center. I was only seventeen. I couldn't have my cologne because it had alcohol in it. They kept my hairdryer and said they would return it after it was inspected. They took my clothes and gave me what amounted to nothing more than pajamas. I was not allowed to be in my room during the day. I had to stay in the commons area within eyesight of the nurse's station.

In the pale, muted colors of institutional furniture, the kind easily cleaned when someone vomits on it, was a couch and a few chairs. Because I was still a juvenile, I was housed with other kids my age and would spend two weeks being evaluated. After that, I would be moved to another wing of the facility called "Primary" and would spend my remaining two weeks of inpatient treatment there. In Primary, the population was a mixture of juveniles and adults.

I awoke the first morning not being fully aware of where I was. Someone was banging on my door, telling me it was time to get up and get out of my room. I went to breakfast. There I saw a very cute, short girl my age. Her head was down as she walked determinedly back to her room.

"Excuse me. Could I borrow a hairdryer?" I asked as politely as possible. "I haven't gotten mine back yet."

"Sure!" she replied in a friendly voice that had a pronounced southern accent.

"My name is Rob."

"I'm Amy."

Amy had arrived from Ashland, Kentucky, to visit her mother, who was in treatment there. After a family group session, Amy stayed for treatment as well. Amy was moved to Primary within days of my arrival, so I wasn't able to spend time getting to know her in our group sessions.

I was a kid, arrested in my emotional development. Even though I had requested to go to treatment, I didn't know what to do once I was there. I had no idea how to get at the shit that was festering deep within me, the stuff that was slowly eating me alive, coming out sideways and showing itself as anger and pain, all balled up. I was lashing out at those around me, but I was also turning my shame and guilt inward, punishing myself for how I'd coped with the things in my life over which I'd had no control.

In group, I talked about my family and Bill. I talked about staying at the babysitter's house when I was very young and the loneliness I felt. What I didn't talk about was my sexual assault. I didn't avoid talking about it or hide it. It wasn't close enough in my awareness to do either of those things. It was still so far away, I never saw it, so I didn't talk about it. Surely, it hadn't happened to me but to someone else.

After an evening of what we saw as fun and games, acting like we were getting high, I was told I would be staying in evaluation an extra week because I wasn't getting it. I was pecking at the surface. I wasn't getting at the source of what was going on inside me. But I didn't understand how to get to the root of my problem.

Following three weeks of being evaluated, I was moved to Primary, where I got to see Amy again. After a couple of days, she was released to a halfway house in town, but we stayed in communication after she left. I enjoyed her company and her insights, and she accepted me in all my emotional intensity. I was sad that she would eventually be returning to Kentucky.

I was still in a relationship with Lori, and she visited often. Knowing that an older woman was interested in me made me feel significant, wanted, and loved. I certainly didn't share in group that I was dating a married woman. It was another secret I kept.

As dysfunctional as it was, my intimacy with Lori was the most significant relationship I had. And it was the longest intimate relationship I'd been in. I saw no future in it, but I needed to feel significant to someone. I loved her and didn't want the relationship to end.

After treatment, I returned to my brother's house and attended AA meetings. I saw my friend Amy as often as possible, usually at meetings, but our relationship wasn't a romantic one. She was my best friend. I didn't get a sponsor, as AA said I should. I had Amy, and I didn't want a male sponsor. Without understanding why, I didn't allow men into my inner circle.

Once I started my senior year of high school, I did my best to improve my grades and my attitude for a while. I attended a support group that had been set up by my school counselor, and I made an attempt at playing a school sport—hockey. The other kids had been playing hockey most of their lives, but it was my first attempt at it. It didn't go well, but at least I tried something new.

The support group I was part of in high school was given opportunities to speak with younger school kids about the dangers of substance abuse. I was also given the opportunity to speak with parents about what it was like to be a struggling child. Those early public speaking opportunities gave me a taste of what it is like to teach from stage. I found it easy and I enjoyed sharing.

The only person who knew I was seeing Lori was Leslie, a neighbor of my mom who lived across the street from her. I'd spent a lot of time there before I moved in with

Geoff, and I continued to see them when I could after I moved. I was accepted into the fold of their family—the family I never had, complete with a mom, dad, and three siblings. They too were a bit dysfunctional, but they were a softer place to land when I needed some grounding. I loved and appreciated them. Leslie's husband, Ron, was a teacher at my high school, and I took drafting class just so I could be in his class.

I had a crush on their oldest daughter, but she was younger than me and didn't share my infatuation. I rode skateboard and played frisbee with their middle son. He was a talented hockey player and made it look really easy. That and was probably what led to trying my hand at the sport.

Without talking with me about it first, Leslie went to Lori and told her that if she didn't stop seeing me, she would tell her husband. Lori ended our relationship, which devastated me. I was angry that Leslie had pressured Lori, but I eventually realized that she was intervening for my wellbeing, just as a good parent would. It was the right thing to do. Nothing good was going to come of my relationship with Lori.

The day after I turned eighteen, I moved out of my brother's house. I was eager to get out on my own and desperate to be out from under any authority. They had been wonderful to me, but I needed freedom. It was a chance for me to run, and I did. I had a little money from a part-time job, so I moved into a mobile home in a trailer park with Rick, a guy I had met at AA, and we split the rent.

Now that I was living on my own, I didn't need anybody's permission to skip school, and I frequently did. When school officials asked for a note from my parents explaining why I wasn't at school the day before, I defiantly wrote a note in front of them and told them I didn't live with my parents.

During my senior year, I joined a rock and roll band that was looking for a singer. They weren't an established band, just a group of guys who wanted to do something more and had formed a garage band. Not long after I joined the band, they found another singer who had a higher range. Dave was a wonderful and energetic kid with a great voice. He could sing songs that we really wanted to play but which required a much higher range than I could sing. Dave certainly was that voice. I found a way to stay in the group and add value by buying a small synthesizer. I sang a few songs and played keyboards on a few others.

When we started playing in bars, I needed to make a decision. I was an eighteen-year-old recovering alcoholic with less than a year of sobriety. I enjoyed playing in the band and wanted to continue, but I also understood the value of being sober and how close I was to being in trouble by spending time in bars. I decided that if I started to feel a pull to drink, I would quit the band. I was very open about my situation with the other bandmates, and they were all considerate and supportive. Some of them were getting high when we were together, but they never did it in front of me. I was grateful for their understanding.

I got kicked out of my English class senior year, and that almost cost me my diploma. It wasn't pretty, but I was able to pull it together and graduated. My dad made it to my graduation ceremony and stayed afterward long enough to give me some small appliances as gifts: a blender, a popcorn popper, and a small deep fryer. Then he left. I was shocked and happy that he'd come, but in the busyness and excitement of the day, I didn't give him the attention I should have for putting forth the effort to come.

Following her own graduation, my treatment buddy, Amy, moved back to Kentucky and to her longtime boyfriend, John. John had always seemed to be a source of trouble for her, and I was afraid for my friend when I learned she would be continuing her relationship with him. I loved her dearly and wanted only the best for her. We spoke often on the phone, sharing our joys, fears, and troubles, including our relationship challenges and failings. We relied on each other. My feelings for Amy became complicated. I hadn't had a close female friend since Judy Green, so functional, nonsexual relationships with girls my age were foreign to me. But I did my best to keep my feelings about her in check.

I met two important people during my time in the band. One of them was Dean, our sound man. Rick moved out of our mobile home the summer after graduation, and I needed a roommate because I struggled to pay the rent by myself on the few dollars I made working at Hardee's. I was grateful when Dean moved in.

We were a good fit. He liked to laugh and have fun, and like me, he was a sensitive soul. We were both financially strapped and often relied on our parents to provide food for us. It was always good news when one of us was invited home for dinner. That was usually Dean. Dean's mom cooked a lot of food, which meant she would send the leftovers home with him. Our usual meals of corn flakes and milk were replaced with home-cooked meals, at least for a few days. Life was good.

Dean wasn't much of a drinker and I didn't drink at all. We didn't throw parties at the Taj Mahal of a mobile home we lived in, so it was quite a surprise when we were evicted from that palace for throwing a loud, drunken party. I called Geoff, who was dabbling with student rentals, and told him what had happened. He allowed Dean and I to move into one of his empty rentals and helped me take my previous landlord to court.

Geoff called some inspector contacts he had, and the trailer Dean and I had been living in was soon condemned as unfit for human habitation. In court I was able to get back all the rent I had paid because a landlord couldn't rent out an unfit property.

The second important figure I met that summer was Paula, who was a friend of our drummer. We started seeing each other on a regular basis. She was my first actual girlfriend of my own age, and I could tell others about her because, for once, I didn't have to hide a relationship. I had become adept at hiding relationships, whether it was my relationship to alcohol and drugs, a relationship with a schoolteacher, or a relationship with a married woman. I was free to be in this relationship, and I felt that freedom. I acted upon that freedom. Within months, Paula was pregnant.

8

I was terrified. I was only eighteen years old and I was going to be father. I had no idea what a father was because I had no well of knowledge to draw my bucket from. For the majority of my life, my own father had been unable to say I love you, give a hug, or show any emotion at all. My stepfather had come in from out of nowhere and tried to rule with an iron fist.

My older brothers were the closest thing I had to male role models, but despite their best loving efforts, I had been so caught up in my own shit, I was barely aware of their influence, let alone in a position to learn anything from them. Running had been my modus operandi: Run from pain. Run from rejection before I could be rejected. Run toward any unknown that had to be better than where I'd been. Run toward relationships with women because I needed to fill a hole within.

I couldn't run from this. I had to run toward it. I was responsible for bringing a life into this world. Paula and I moved in together and did our best to provide a stable family environment for the birth of our child. We moved into the upstairs apartment of a duplex in Altoona, not far from Paula's parents, who lived only a few blocks from their own parents. I knew I needed to make more money, and when I saw an advertisement for a job at Sears, I applied.

I was hired on the maintenance team. Arriving at the store incredibly early in the morning, I scraped gum and heel marks from floors as well as swept, mopped, and waxed them. I was quickly becoming an expert in floor care. It wasn't how I envisioned my life, but I was making more money than I had been slinging burgers and fries.

Soon after being hired, I was transferred to the warehouse. The hours were better and it was a bit of a pay raise. I enjoyed working with customers, getting them their orders, and helping them get large boxes secured to small vehicles. I often cringed as they left, fingers crossed that the load I had done my best to secure to their vehicle at least made it out of the parking lot before slipping through my best knot tying efforts and hitting the pavement.

It was a beautiful, emotional day when Nicole Dawn entered this world. I cried seeing Paula go through so much pain, and I worried about my child, who was desperately trying to enter this world. I helped deliver her and cut the cord. Then I held her and was in complete awe. Her tiny body and presence in the world were amazing in every way possible. She was perfect, and I was instantly in love. I kept the scrub top I was wearing the moment she was born. It smelled like her, and I never wanted to lose that. I returned to the shirt often and buried my face in it to smell my child at the moment of her birth and feel the love and amazement I felt that day. I had done something remarkable and significant: I had cocreated the most precious and beautiful life that had ever been brought into the world.

The morning of her birth, I purchased a local paper when I left the hospital because I wanted a newspaper from the day she was born. I knew my life was never going to be the same, and I wanted to memorialize that day. I put it away someplace safe to eventually give to her.

Nicole was my world. I couldn't get enough time with her and I couldn't get close enough to her. Someone gave us a papoose sling, and I would tuck her in it, secure her little body close to mine, and do all the household chores I needed to do. My hands were free to do laundry and dishes, and I could see her perfect, peaceful, angelic little face whenever I looked down. As I cared for and loved Nicole, I felt I had a purpose. I had an amazing child I was responsible for. I was her protector. I was her dad.

With the birth of my daughter, my own father felt the need to finally act. He did something he had never done before. Unannounced, he came to visit me. As I was finishing my shift at work, a friend told me that a man who said he was my father was there to see me. I was so confused, I thought it had to be my brother Geoff. My dad would *not* drop in to see me. He lived hours south of Eau Claire—certainly not a drive to make on a whim.

As I walked out to the parking lot, I saw his car and knew it was him. But I had no idea why he was there and felt a sense of dread as I approached his car. I opened the door and sat down in the passenger seat. After a couple of pleasantries, he told me why he was there. "Now that you're a father yourself, I think it's important for you to know the truth about your own paternity."

The words entered my ears like mud trying to flow through a screen.

"I'm not your father," he said.

"What?" I couldn't wrap my brain around his revelation and didn't know what to say. "Why would you say that? What makes you believe that?" I needed proof. What he gave me that day made no sense, and in my mind, it certainly did not back up his claim.

"You didn't look like the other kids when you were born, and when I went to pay the hospital bill, it had already been paid."

"That's it? That's why you believe you're not my father!" I exclaimed.

"I'm not your father."

"If you're not my father, then who is?"

"Bill Armson"

I was speechless. I had lived with the man, hated the man, and screamed at the man, "You're not my father!" How could it possibly be true that he was my biological father?

Dad and I concluded our talk, and I immediately went to see Mom in search of answers. When I arrived, Mom was home alone.

"I just had a very interesting conversation with Dad."

"Oh, really?"

"Yes. He claims he's not my father and that Bill is. Is that true?"

"That's ridiculous," she said with no emotion.

"So, it's not true?" I asked, being as direct and serious as I could.

"That's ridiculous," she repeated.

It wasn't a denial and it wasn't an affirmation of what Dad had said. It wasn't a yes and it wasn't a no. It was a vague response that told me nothing. I wondered if it was possible that I'd been lied to all those years.

Who was I? Where had I come from? My brothers were not my brothers? Was I really the child of a long-term affair? Had I been lied to my entire life? Who else knew about it? Was it true or was it just the speculation of a bitter, divorced man? My mind raced. He clearly believed he was not my father. I wondered if that was why he had been so distant my entire life and treated me like an inconvenience.

I refused to give in to the dark pull that was attempting to suffocate me. With my father's revelations, the foundation of my world had been rocked. It also affected my relationship at home with Paula and my daughter.

We learn from those around us. I learned how to be a father from my parents, and my education on that was sparse. The clearing of my father's conscience stripped away what little confidence I had to be there for Nicole and her mother. I had no idea what I was doing.

At the same time, I knew I needed some sort of career. I had a beautiful little girl to provide for, and I knew I had to make more money. I had a driving need to serve and a need to be significant. Maybe they were one and the same. My life needed purpose. I respected police officers and saw them coming to the aid of people who needed help. They protected innocent people. Police officers did for others what hadn't been done for me.

I enrolled in a two-year police science program at the local technical college. I didn't do well at juggling all that was going on in my life and became very selfish, only focusing on myself and keeping my head above water. My home life suffered.

Paula and I often fought, and it affected my relationship with my daughter. I was tense and irritable. I had no idea how to be a father. Because of my own childhood, I didn't even know what a father was. And clearly, I had no idea how to be in a committed relationship.

I was lying to both myself and Paula. We weren't good for each other. I was the furthest thing from healthy as I could be. I was twenty-one months sober when Nicole was born, but I had not begun to dig deep into the traumas that were unconsciously shaping my life and my actions. Those traumas were running my life and every decision I made. The wounded child in me took over anytime there was a threat, real or perceived. My innocent daughter was paying the price for my inability to get control of my life and heal my traumas.

I wasn't sure who I'd been before my father's revelations and my mother's inability to give me a straight answer. It felt as though I had no foundation to stand on. Who was my biological father? What did it mean to be a father? What was the difference between being a father and being a dad? I was certainly Nicole's father, but what the hell did it mean to be her dad? I had never experienced a dad in my own life, and now there was a very real possibility that all I had believed to be true was actually a lie. Feeling betrayed and abandoned, I resorted to my best self-preservation tactic: I ran.

Paula and I split, and I moved into Mom and Bill's basement, which was the last place I wanted to be.

The moment any woman paid attention to me, I had a distraction to help me avoid healing the festering wounds that were interfering with all my relationships. I met Amanda where she worked as manager of the Sears portrait studio. I would see her when I was bringing merchandise from the warehouse to the sales floor. She was a bit exotic, very adventurous, and loved photography like I did. She had her own home and a young son. We started to hang out, and our relationship soon turned intimate.

Amanda had a troubled past full of physical abuse, betrayal, and hurt. She'd lived with a foster mother, Cindy, who had been very kind to her. Cindy was still in Amanda's life and worked for the State of Wisconsin. During a conversation with Amanda, Cindy made an offhand comment about the state building a new maximum security prison in Portage, my hometown. She suggested we apply for jobs as correctional officers.

Since starting my relationship with Amanda, I had focused more on her than on school, and my grades had suffered. The thought of getting a job in the prison system, which was technically in law enforcement, was appealing. The pay was tremendously better than what I was making at Sears, and I considered it a career instead of just a job. Plus, it had a retirement package. Amanda and I both applied and we were both hired.

We had to successfully complete the Corrections Training Academy in Oshkosh before we could work at a Wisconsin prison. Amanda was slated to start the seven-week training academy first. I was to begin in the following class. Training was Monday through Friday. Friday evenings, she made the three-hour drive back to Eau Claire for the weekend, and she returned to Oshkosh Sunday afternoons.

As she approached the end of her training, we knew we were moving, we just didn't know where. Toward the end of her last week of class, she would find out which prison she was being assigned to, and she would be expected to start work the following Monday. We had one weekend to pack, find a place to live, and move. As the final weekend approached, I was busy packing up the house, renting a moving truck, and getting everything ready for a move to an unknown destination somewhere in Wisconsin.

The news came. She was assigned to Columbia Correctional Institution (CCI) in Portage. We were going back to the town of my birth. I was moving away from my daughter and away from my family with a woman I had only been involved with for a few months. What could possibly go wrong?

I found a house to rent in Pardeeville, which was eight miles from Portage. My friend Dean and I began making trips from Eau Claire to Pardeeville with our belongings. Friday evening, Amanda returned from Oshkosh to Eau Claire, and we made the final trip together to our new home with the last of our belongings. The following Monday, she began working at CCI.

9

I was excited to start my career with the Wisconsin Department of Corrections. My training in Oshkosh was regimented. It included a set schedule of classroom work with physical training several days a week that included push-ups, sit-ups, running, and self-defense training. One classmate would dress up in the huge padded suit and we would take turns learning to use a baton on them.

We learned compliance holds and takedown procedures. We had weapons training that included handguns, shotguns, and rifles. We learned the concept of escalating force and when to use deadly force.

Columbia Correctional Institution was a newly open maximum security prison. What they actually called it was a supermax prison. CCI would be getting the worst of the worst inmates from around the state, and when I called home from school, I heard from Amanda just how dangerous the inmate population was there.

I did well in school, and I won an award in my human relations class for my abilities to deescalate conflicts and work with inmates. I felt I had a purpose, was good at something, and could make a difference if given the opportunity to use my human relations skills rather than a deadly weapon.

On weekends I came home to spend time with Amanda. On one of my last weekends home before I graduated, I saw the parts of the coffee maker in the kitchen sink but failed to grasp their meaning. Amanda didn't drink coffee.

As I approached the end of my training, I requested to be assigned to CCI with Amanda, and when I graduated, my request was granted. At twenty-one, I was a brand-new corrections officer.

Working in a maximum security prison was surreal. There were people incarcerated there I'd heard about on TV, humans who had done unspeakable acts of violence to other human beings. There were a few inmates I felt were closer to the animal world than to the human species, and that was being unkind to the animals. CCI was a world within a world. It was a population of people the outside world no longer wanted to see or deal with.

Also housed there were people who had made very tragic mistakes due to addiction and were now paying a tremendous price for their actions. There were inmates I would have enjoyed spending time with if they hadn't been incarcerated. Other than having been convicted of a crime, they were like me.

I understood and always respected my boundaries with the inmates in my care, and I fully understood that my job in the prison didn't include punishing the inmates. The court system had already handed out their punishment. The greatest right they'd had—their freedom—had been taken from them. My job was the safe care, custody, and control of inmates for whom I had responsibility. Not all of my fellow officers saw their job as I did.

Some of my coworkers believed they had the right to torment and antagonize the inmates. They passed judgment on them because of the nature of their crimes and treated them in a way that instigated physical confrontations. It was dangerous for us as well as the inmates, but those corrections officers seemed to get off on the power trip.

CCI was still in the process of opening, and every day, the total number of inmates in the prison rose as housing units opened. The days were busy, filled with routine, and sprinkled with fights, cell searches, and discovered drugs. Under my breath, I often said, "What the hell!"

About a month into my new career, I returned home in the evening to find Amanda already in bed but not yet asleep.

"I'm in love with someone else, and I need to see if it's going to work," she said, blindsiding me. That revelation was followed by, "You need to find another place to live."

Ah, yes. The coffee maker.

Amanda's lover, Ed, was married and had children. He also worked at CCI—on the same shift as Amanda and me. I had worked side by side with Ed as he was having an affair with my girlfriend. I moved out of the house I had found for us only a few weeks earlier. He left his wife and kids and moved in with Amanda.

I left with some clothes, a bowl, a plate, a knife, a fork, a spoon, and a radio that also played cassette tapes. After a short stay with a coworker, I rented an apartment that was as cold and empty as I felt inside.

I felt like a fool. I had been played and betrayed. The sounds of my radio playing my new anthem, "Nobody's Fool" by the band Cinderella, echoed within the empty walls and hardwood floors. The landlord was kind enough to give me a bed—well, actually just the box spring that sat directly on the floor.

At the start of my shift each morning, I had to sit in a meeting that included Amanda and Ed. I couldn't have made myself any smaller in that room. I did my best to be invisible, swallowing my feelings of hurt and rejection as best I could, often failing.

I often cried on the shoulder of my brother Kip, who was now living in Seattle. He could hear how badly I wanted Amanda back and gave me emphatic instructions to get a dog. I found Katie at a breeder on a return trip to Eau Claire. She was a black Labrador puppy that filled my life with joy. I had never raised a dog from puppyhood before I started training Katie. It was a great bonding experience as well as a distraction from the emotional chaos that surrounded me.

Three weeks after Ed left his wife and moved in with Amanda, he moved back home. Following Ed's departure, Amanda called with car trouble almost two hours from home and asked me to come get her. Kip was in town, and sadly, I ended my visit with him to rush off to rescue the woman who had betrayed me.

Strangely, during the ride back to Amanda's, she made no mention of my new puppy in the back seat. When I delivered Amanda to her house, she said she wanted to reconcile our relationship, but I blew right past a giant red flag when she became furious that I had gotten a dog. She screamed so loudly at me that Katie was so scared, she urinated on the floor. Amanda had literally scared the piss out of the dog with her screaming. Unfortunately, it didn't scare me, and it should have. We got back together.

Amanda and I found a new duplex to rent in Portage, and we moved back in together. What I didn't see until well after the fact was that during my obsession with Amanda and all the drama that was surrounding our relationship, I was slowly pulling away from Nicole.

Nicole's mother was dating a man I went to high school with. He was in the crowd that bullied me, liked to pick fights with me, and generally did their best to show me how worthless my life was. He smoked pot then, and to my knowledge, he still smoked pot. Paula appeared happy with him and the life they were creating together.

I didn't see that I was allowing Amanda to slowly isolate me from my family. I was so emotionally immature and craving of acceptance from anyone who would give it to me that I didn't notice what was happening. I had made Amanda my entire world. If *we* were okay, *I* was okay.

Amanda and I decided to get married, but I didn't tell my family. No one attended the ceremony except two of our friends, Gina and LeRoy, and they served as our witnesses.

About the same time, my friend Dean, who was still living just outside the city limits of Eau Claire, joined a volunteer fire department. As he was telling me about it, I found myself feeling a pull of purpose deep within me. I remembered the days of following the fire trucks with Mom and how I looked up to those brave souls.

Soon after, I walked into the fire station in Portage and requested an application. My application was accepted and I became a volunteer firefighter—the beginning of what would become a thirty-year career in the fire service that would change my life.

I began my training and was issued my first set of gear that consisted of a long black coat and boots that came up to my thighs. They were out of date before I was ever issued them. More senior members were issued modern gear, but new recruits got the older gear. Soon I was responding to calls and riding in the fire engines—every kid's dream.

Not long after I started as a volunteer with the fire department, the owner of Portage Ambulance Service came to one of our Tuesday night training sessions and gave a presentation. He was looking for people who might be interested in becoming emergency medical technicians and want to work as volunteers for his service. I jumped at the chance and told Amanda about it. She wanted to join as well.

We took the training to become licensed EMTs in the State of Wisconsin. We could now begin taking shifts and going on calls. We were issued radios and pagers, along with our bright orange ambulance smocks and jackets, all bearing the name Portage Ambulance Service.

One snowy afternoon, our two-person crew was dispatched to a cardiac arrest on the north side of town. The heart of an elderly, frail woman had stopped. It was the first time I ever did CPR on a human. I never forgot that call. It was my first patient who died. In EMT school, they made it sound like we could save them all. If we showed up and did what we were trained to do, patients would be saved, not die. That wasn't the case. I learned that day that people would sometimes die in my hands.

Amanda and I were creating a life together in Portage, and I thought we were past the events that had led to the breakup before our marriage. I thought being in a dysfunctional relationship was better than being alone, and I was doing my best to not create conflict at all cost.

We had forged a bond when we worked together at the prison, and now we were working together on the ambulance as volunteers. But making Amanda the center of my world meant that my world was getting smaller. At the same time, the arguments between us were increasing and becoming more rageful. I did what I could to appease

Amanda. There were fewer fights when I did, and by avoiding conflict, I wasn't exposed to her rages. She was also less likely to leave, and I didn't want her to leave because I didn't want to be alone. It felt like a matter of self-preservation, so I kept the peace at home at all costs.

I missed being a father to Nicole, but I had convinced myself at some superficial level that Nicole was better off with her new family rather than being pulled back and forth between Paula and me. I thought Nicole was safer away from the turmoil unfolding in my life that I wasn't strong enough to stop, but at the same time, I felt guilt and shame for not being in her life more.

I missed being a father so badly that I wanted Amanda to get pregnant, and a year after our marriage she did. A little less than five years after Nicole's birth, my second daughter, Danielle, entered the world. Just as the world had changed for me with Nicole's birth, it did with the birth of Danielle too. The light got lighter and the dark became more vile.

I cherished my time with Danielle, but my time with Amanda was descending into chaos as she became more rageful and her outbursts turned violent. I felt powerless to stop it, and in my state of emotional insecurity, not only did I not stop it, I made it worse. I was at the mercy of my emotions. I was triggered frequently by the fighting. My fear of abandonment kept me stuck in an extremely unhealthy relationship. We were both emotionally wounded, and we were dealing with each other from those wounded places.

Danielle brought stability and focus to my life. I felt unconditional love for her, and because she was an infant, she actually needed me. I wasn't at risk of being abandoned by her. The only person who could take her away from me was Amanda.

We now had something else to fight over. I could feel Amanda doing her best to rip Danielle away from me, just as she could probably feel me trying to rip Danielle away from her. We both needed our child for the same unhealthy reason: to fill an emptiness within us that no one else could fill, not even Danielle, because it could only be filled from within ourselves.

The first time Amanda punched me was during an argument in the bedroom. With a closed fist, she drew back to strike me and I turned away from her to avoid the incoming blows. She left bruises on my back in several places. I told Danielle's babysitters, Gina and LeRoy, what had happened. I was ashamed that I had been hit, but I wanted someone to know about it. And I showed them the bruises because I wanted them to know I wasn't lying.

I began to see Amanda's aggressive tendencies, once only directed at me, turn toward our daughter. I couldn't stand by and simply watch, so I did what I could to shield my daughter from her mother. Amanda began using corporal punishment as a way of disciplining Danielle, and I was stunned. Corporal punishment with anger as the underlying tone was the rule of law in our house now, not love. She was using physical punishment to make her point known to both of us.

I feared for my daughter's safety and needed to protect her. It was becoming clear that I had to leave with my daughter, and I began to quietly stash a little money in a file cabinet for the day when that would happen.

I finally found the courage to leave following a particularly intense fight. Amanda raged and threatened violence against Danielle and me. When I attempted to call the police, she tried to rip the phone from my hand. I left the house and went to the police station, but when I returned with a police officer, Amanda refused to let either them or me in. Eventually, Amanda allowed the police in but not me. The officer eventually allowed me in, but only to retrieve some personal items and my cash. I pleaded with the officer to allow me to leave with my daughter, but that didn't happen. The fact that I couldn't do what I set out to do—keep my daughter safe by leaving with her—left me devastated and in disbelief. How could they not see what was happening? The system was failing me.

After gathering a few items of clothing, I went to the file cabinet to get my cash, about two hundred dollars. It was all gone. I turned to Amanda and demanded my cash.

"What cash?" she asked smugly.

With no cash and only a few clothes, I left my wife, my daughter, and my dog. I had been stripped of everything again, including my dignity, and I was an emotional mess: angry, frustrated, defeated, embarrassed, and hurt. To an outside observer, such as the police, my emotions no doubt looked like anger. And I probably looked as unhinged as I was accusing Amanda of being.

I crashed with a guy I worked with at the prison. Within a few days, a new friend, Joe, said he was renting a new place. He invited me to move in with him. Joe had recently started at the fire department, and the apartment was right across the street from the fire station.

I filed for divorce and petitioned the court for full custody of my daughter. Amanda did everything she could to stop me. During the course of the divorce, Amanda accused me of child neglect. After a short interview with the sheriff's deputy and an attorney, it was obvious I hadn't done anything wrong, and I never heard any more about the accusation.

I felt under attack and lived in a constant state of being triggered. Someone once said you should trust the teacher that is the trigger, but I wasn't ready to absorb the valuable lessons that were being shown to me.

As the court proceedings progressed, I made attempts to move on with my life. I wanted a life with my daughter, and I believed the perfect partner would fill the pain that lived within me. I still hadn't learned the lesson that my perceived emptiness couldn't be filled by another relationship.

If I just found the right person, I believed all would be right in the world. My attempt to fill my internal wounds with external solutions was not the answer, and yet I tried. I was still a long way from understanding that I needed to heal myself.

10

I could be a hero at the fire department. I mattered because I was responding to other people's emergencies. I showed up and saved the day. At the same time, I was always on guard. I had an internal dialog that said I was a fraud, that I was just building myself up by using my role as a first responder, and sooner or later someone would figure it out. Being a volunteer member of the fire department was another attempt to fill my need to be seen and appreciated.

Living across the street from the station made it easy to get on a first-out truck when there was a call. That way, I was among the first on scene, which was where all the action was. It was also exciting to now be riding the trucks that Mom and I followed when I was a child.

Living in a small town with people I knew and responding to my neighbors' emergencies made it likely I would eventually respond to a scene involving someone I knew. My fire department pager jolted me awake one morning. The dispatch was for a single-vehicle accident on Highway 33 just outside of town. I made it onto the first truck out.

With sirens blaring, our flashing lights pierced the darkness and reflected off the passing houses as we sped to the crash. My seat on the truck that morning was called a jump seat, and it faced backwards. Because of that, I was unable to see anything ahead of us as we approached the crash. We were the first to arrive on scene, getting there even before law enforcement. We came to a stop and I jumped off the truck with no visual warning of the magnitude of the crash or what I was about to do. There was no time to put the jumbled pieces together and begin to process what I was seeing, and there was no time to prepare for what was about to happen.

The destroyed two-door hatchback car, illuminated only by the lights from our fire engine, had crashed head-on into the solid steel guardrail on a short bridge. There were no signs that the driver had hit his brakes before the collision, and he'd hit the steel and concrete barrier at highway speed, coming to an instantaneous and devastating stop.

I noted that the car hatchback was open and made my way to the driver's side. The door was also open, and I saw a woman's body in an unlikely position in the back seat. Her legs were in the hatch area and her hips were draped over the top of the back seat. Her blonde hair gently draped across the seat where she had been sitting, and her face was turned toward me, her lifeless eyes staring at me. There was a hole in the center of her forehead, and her brain was coming out of the hole. She had been killed instantly.

The driver's seat had broken and was twisted toward the door, and the driver was moaning and moving. The front seat passenger was not moving, so I turned my attention to him next. I came to the passenger side of the car and found an unconscious man wearing a crisp, clean, white undershirt. Around his neck hung a green glowing necklace, the kind you might get at a fair. His lower lip was split open, and there was a small amount of blood on his shirt near the collar. His left lower leg had an open fracture with his leg bone exposed. I couldn't tell if he was breathing, so I rubbed my knuckles into his chest and yelled at him in hope of rousing a response. Nothing.

In that moment, the driver, still in his seat with his back to me, said, "Rob, I'm hurt bad." I recognized his voice, and time stopped.

Slowly, the pieces fell together like dominoes. If the driver was Garth, then the man I had been trying to arouse in the front seat was Tom, Garth's roommate. Garth and I had gone to school together. The three of us had worked together at the prison, and I knew them well. The empty eyes that stared at me from the back seat belonged to Garth's sometimes girlfriend, Terri. The force of the crash had slammed her body forward and then backward against the hatchback, opening it.

When I met Terri, she was ending her relationship with Garth. I was in my divorce process with Amanda and found Terri's kindness, compassion, and positive outlook on life refreshing. We spent many late nights sharing our dreams and aspirations for lives we were not yet living. Terri was an oasis in the chaos that surrounded me. For a brief time, we were lovers, but after a few weeks, it became apparent that our intimate time together was coming to an end. Her head told her Garth wasn't good for her, but her heart wouldn't let her walk away. I helped her make the choice by ending our relationship three weeks before the accident that took her life.

As a professional with a job to do at the scene, I knew I had to keep working. I could not afford to be distracted by my emotions. Tom couldn't afford to have me distracted. I might be able to save his life, but only if I focused. We got Tom's limp, mangled body out of the car and into the ambulance that had joined us at the scene. And as the EMT initiating care at the scene, I hopped into the ambulance and accompanied him to the hospital. We were only a few minutes from the hospital when Tom's heart stopped. I started chest compressions in a vain attempt to keep him alive long enough to get him to the hospital, where I would have help saving him. His life slipped away beneath my hands.

Not long after arriving at the hospital, the emergency department staff stopped their resuscitation efforts. Garth survived, but Tom and Terri were both gone.

In the weeks that followed the accident, I asked myself some painful questions: Was Terri in the car with Garth that morning because I had broken up with her? Did she go back to him because I ended our relationship?

Nightmares became a normal visitor. I was afraid to go to sleep and did everything I could to avoid it. I was exhausted and felt a scream inside me—like the one I'd felt inside when I was fourteen—that could not find its way to the surface. It was trapped within me, waiting to explode, like a hand wrapped around a firecracker.

I stayed out late and had trouble getting up for work. I was late several times. My bosses were both understanding and angry. They weren't sure what to do with me. They knew the trouble I was having with Amanda in the divorce process, and they had trouble with her too. They knew what had happened with Garth and Tom and knew I'd been there with Tom when he died. I still had a job to do, but I wasn't doing it well.

Amanda did her best to capitalize on the place of despair I found myself in. Pushing me to the edge and watching me publicly disintegrate would be the best thing for her and her case to keep custody of Danielle. My falling apart would take the focus off all the things she had done.

One night when Amanda and I were both working an overtime shift in the towers at the prison, she laughed out loud and said that there were other officers making bets to see when I would hang myself from one of the guard towers. They weren't far from being right. I *had* been contemplating suicide. I still missed Amanda, despite everything, and I felt ridiculous for doing so. I had been rejected. Old wounds had been reopened. During depositions, I learned that Amanda was seeing another man from the prison, and in fact, they were already living together. She had moved on, but I really hadn't.

Days blended into weeks and fell into months. Meetings with attorneys about my ongoing custody battle meant spending money I didn't have. It was becoming clear I was fighting a losing battle. I knew the truth about what had happened in our marriage, but I could not find a way to bring that truth to light. I wanted Danielle with me and I wanted her away from Amanda's daily influence. I didn't want her to become her mother's daughter. Danielle was sweet and innocent, a kindhearted soul. Amanda was vindictive and physically, emotionally, and verbally abusive—all things I wanted to protect my daughter from.

The court date for my divorce was set. I would have an opportunity to say to the court and the world what had been happening. Judge Charles was hearing our case. I didn't know him personally, but I knew he was stern and had been on the bench for years. I prayed he would see through the lies and manipulation. I felt betrayed, and not only did I hope the court would see that I was the victim, I hoped the court would see the need to protect Danielle from Amanda as much as I did. I needed an advocate.

Two days had actually been set aside for our trial. Before the close of the first day, my attorney had presented my side of the case. Afterward, Judge Charles began by saying, "So we don't waste any more of the court's time . . . ."

There it was. My fight to protect my daughter was seen as a waste of the court's time. I felt defeated and humiliated. Primary physical placement stayed with Amanda and I had visitation rights. Danielle would be with each of us on alternating holidays. I had lost the fight for my daughter. The assassination of my character had been complete. In the judge's ruling, he stated he believed physical abuse had been perpetrated by both parties. He believed her lies.

The dog I had brought into my life when Amanda and I were separated was ordered to stay with the *family* because it was the *family pet*. To dump salt in the wound, the shotgun that I had purchased for $325 from Amanda's now live-in boyfriend before he had that distinction would remain with Amanda until I paid the remainder of the money I owed Amanda from the divorce settlement, which, ironically, was $325.

At the time of the hearing, I was an emotional wreck from the accident aftermath I had witnessed. If the accident that had taken the lives of my friends hadn't happened so close to my final hearing, could I have been in a more emotionally stable place to intelligently argue a case for my daughter? Could I have argued my case from a place of facts instead of from a place of such volatile emotions?

Upon hearing the news of my losses, my roommate immediately took me to the bank. He cashed the paycheck he'd just received that day, which was a fraction over the funds I needed to pay Amanda, and gave it to me. Then he ordered me to call Amanda and tell her I was coming to pay her and get the shotgun. Joe's kindness was a small victory in an otherwise very dark day. And my dark days weren't over yet.

11

At work, I took the promotional exam for sergeant and passed. Several hundred officers had taken the exam and I had scored twelfth in the state. Those at the top of the list got more interview opportunities than those at the bottom. I had interviews in several institutions around the state and had offers at a couple of them. The thought of moving away from Amanda felt like a glimpse at freedom, a chance to cleanly step into a new life, even though it also meant that I was moving away from Danielle.

I accepted a position as the sergeant coordinating work release at Kenosha Correctional Institution (KCC) in Kenosha, Wisconsin. I'd been seeing a woman named Jennifer for a few months. We'd met only days following the death of my friends. Jennifer owned a beauty salon in Portage and had a troubled five-year-old son named Owen. Because Jennifer owned a business in Portage and her son's father also lived there, I didn't think she would want to go with me to Kenosha, but I knew I would miss her if she didn't come. She was an outgoing woman who laughed a lot. I found that refreshing, considering what I'd been through. But her son was another story. He was a strong-willed child who threw frequent temper tantrums that involved throwing things, screaming, and breaking things. He tested his mother's will on a regular basis.

I was a bit naïve about the seriousness of Owen's behavior, and I wanted the relationship to work. I offered her the opportunity to join me. Much to my surprise, she said yes. Not only was I moving, I was moving in with Jennifer and her very troubled son.

One of my last emergency calls as a volunteer EMT at the Portage Ambulance Service was with my roommate and friend, Joe. We were dispatched to a farm tractor accident. When we arrived, it was painfully clear that there was nothing we could do.

A fifteen-year-old boy had been in a hurry to finish his chores late in the afternoon because it was prom night. He was driving the tractor on the edge of the field on his way back to the house, probably driving faster than he should. I'm sure the rock that was the size of a small car had been on the edge of the field his entire life. He had driven past it more times than he could count. On that sunny afternoon, he struck the sloping rock with the rear tire of the tractor and the tractor flipped over.

The boy's father and a farm hand were standing and talking near the barn. Off in the distance, on the far side of the field, it appeared something was wrong. They could see that the tractor appeared to be upside down and ran across the field to it.

They found the boy beneath the machinery, his head trapped beneath the small fender of the rear wheel and hard earth. When we arrived, footprints in the dirt encircled the tractor where his father had frantically looked for a way to free his son. We could see where he'd dug and clawed in the dirt with his bare hands to free the boy. Once he'd pulled him out, he started CPR in the desperate attempt to save the boy, but he quickly realized there was nothing to be done because the boy's scull had been crushed.

He left his son and walked back to the house to wait at the kitchen table for his wife to return from the grocery store. He needed to tell her that their only child was dead.

Joe stayed with the boy and the medical examiner. I went to the house to sit in silence with the boy's father at their kitchen table until the boy's mother walked through her door and learned that her world would never be the same.

It was another heart-wrenching call that left images I could never unsee. I'd already experienced how fragile human life was through my work as an EMT, but I was reminded of that lesson in a brutal way. In a split second, a boy hurrying to finish his chores so he could get ready for prom could have his life ripped from him. I was becoming more anxious about the fact that not only could I be abandoned by the ending of a relationship, but that death could easily and swiftly take a life from me.

Jennifer and I moved to Somers, Wisconsin, about eight miles from Kenosha, and I joined the Somers Volunteer Fire Department and Ambulance Service. When I wasn't running emergency calls at night or on the weekends, my full-time job was working at a small, minimum security prison—KCC—that was located in a not so nice part of the city. It was normal to see gang activity on the streets that surrounded the prison. The inmates in my charge were from the same streets, some from the very gangs that controlled the neighborhoods I could see from my office window.

My role was to get them jobs outside the prison so they would have some funds to get them started once they were released. Once they were employed, they paid a small amount to the state for room and board.

This contrasted greatly with my previous job at CCI, a maximum security prison where anytime an inmate left the institution, a strict set of procedures had to be followed. The inmates were strip-searched, which included a visual inspection of all body orifices. I had to see *all* orifices. If he was entering the institution, he put on bright orange institutional clothing after the search and was then restrained with handcuffs, waist chains, and leg irons.

But at KCC, I handed an inmate the keys to a state van. He would then drive an entire van load of inmates all over the Kenosha and Racine area, dropping off and picking up inmates at work. With no correctional officer supervision, that driver and all the inmates would return, on their own, to the prison. It took me a while to wrap my head around that.

There were times when the inmates didn't find their way back to the prison after work. That was an escape. We would file the necessary paperwork, which would alert local law enforcement of the escape, and we would carry on. When they were apprehended, they went to the county jail with a new set of charges against them and would then be sent back to a maximum security prison.

A few of the inmates at KCC did want to make lasting changes in their lives and were appreciative of any help I could give them to be better prepared for life after prison. I felt great satisfaction, like I had made a real difference, when I was able to help them secure a good job.

In prison, an inmate could be given a conduct report, or as we called it, a ticket, for just about anything: too many magazines in his cell, speaking in a disrespectful tone to a staff member, or loaning another inmate a cigarette. If an officer had a grudge against an inmate, that officer could find something to write up the inmate.

One inmate in particular had been sentenced to prison for the better part of his adult life for manslaughter. He'd taken the life of another man. By the time I met him, he had spent eighteen years locked up. He was working in minimum security in the KCC kitchen. I found him to be friendly and agreeable. He did his job well and was a good cook and baker in less than ideal conditions.

During his eighteen years behind bars, this man had never been issued a conduct report by an officer. I was amazed. My last act as the work release coordinator at Kenosha Correctional Center was to negotiate an arrangement with one of my favorite bakeries in Racine to secure him a job before his release date. I had never placed an inmate at this bakery before. He was appreciative of the opportunity. I don't know what happened to him, but I did my best to help him succeed outside the system.

My days were lived in two worlds that could intersect without warning. I lived with a pager that could, at any moment, force me into another situation I could never unsee.

The town of Somers was situated between two sets of railroad tracks, one on each end of town. Kenosha County was unique in that all of the roads ran either straight north and south or straight east and west. I had never experienced a train collision with a car before working in Somers. In the short time that I was there, I experienced several.

The freight train engineer said he could see the headlights of two vehicles cutting through the darkness as they approached the railroad crossing. They were coming at a high rate of speed and in his words, "They were racing me to the crossing."

The first car beat him to the crossing, barely making it safely across. The second car was not so lucky and collided with the locomotive.

We arrived to find the train stopped, blocking the crossing. Laying on the centerline of the lane was the driveshaft from the car. Nothing else was in the road, just the driveshaft. About twenty feet from the road and along the tracks lay the crumpled remains of the boy's car. Another forty feet from the car was the body.

His body lay motionless, face down in the grass. The hood of his gray sweatshirt was covering his head. I gently rolled him over to check for signs of life. His golden-blond hair framed his young face. In the center of his forehead was a gaping hole so large I could see the inside of his head. His brain was completely gone. No fragment remained. The inside of his skull was a pearlescent white. Not only was there no blood, there was no remnant or hint of blood. I was looking at the inside of a human's body.

We searched for his brain. We needed to find it so no one else did. We looked inside the car, walked and searched the tall grass, and walked to the front the of the train where the car collided with the engine. Maybe it was stuck to the side at the point of impact. It wasn't. We never found it.

I clipped the young man's obituary from the newspaper because I wanted his photograph. I wanted to have a picture of him alive. I wanted to remember him as a whole and intact person rather the grotesque body I was witness to that night. I needed to replace the image of his mutilated skull with the vision of his young and innocent face.

There was trauma after trauma. It seemed with each passing day, I was faced with another image I couldn't unsee and experience I couldn't forget. The memories of Tom and Terri were always present, and with each traumatic call, I was adding to the mounting darkness growing within me.

I missed my family in Eau Claire. I missed my oldest daughter. I wanted to go back home. The large cities of Kenosha and Racine were not for me. There were too many people and too much crime.

I began looking for a way to get back home. As a state employee, I had lateral transfer rights. If there was a state position open that was in the correct category for me and I had enough seniority, I could put in the necessary paperwork and transfer into that job. For me, the position of conservation warden was a lateral move, and I knew I would love that job. But there was never an opening. Community corrections was another option that seldom had an open seat. It became clear that to get back to my family, I was going to have to make a radical shift.

The more I thought about being a correctional officer for the rest of my working life, the more it became clear I needed to find a new career. Even though there were occasional highlights of fulfillment, more often than not, there was tension, stress, and sadness behind the locked doors of prison. I was charged with the care, custody, and control of a population of people society wanted locked away. Society no longer wanted to see them. The inmates were castaways, and they acted like it. Most, I observed, were not able to rise above their circumstances. Sometimes those circumstances were of their own creation; sometimes they were not.

I was beginning to realize my soul was being fed when I worked as a firefighter and EMT, despite the intensity of some of the calls I responded to. My soul was being depleted when I worked in the prison. The choice was clear.

I began applying for firefighter positions around the state, including Eau Claire. There was an art to the application and hiring process to become a career firefighter. At that time, there were hundreds of applicants for a single position. The trick was to stand out and stand above so many talented and motivated people.

During a year of applications, I received a few interviews but no job offers. I decided the only department I wanted to work for was Eau Claire. I wanted to go home. I researched what specialty teams Eau Claire had. Everyone was a firefighter and everyone was an EMT. No way to stand out there.

I learned that Eau Claire had several EMTs who were trained to the intermediate level. I found a class and began the process of getting that training. When I learned that the Eau Claire Fire Department had an underwater search and recovery team, I went to the local YMCA and acquired my SCUBA certifications. I did whatever I could think of to be the most appealing candidate who showed up.

The next hiring round, I was extended an invitation to interview in Eau Claire and was hired. I was finally going home.

My brothers convinced me to purchase an upper-lower duplex on East Hill that they owned. It had a good rental history, and I could use the income from renting out the other half of the duplex to make my house payments. I wouldn't even have to get approved for a loan because my brothers would carry it. It was a great idea with just one complication: It was an old house that had been built in stages for twenty years beginning in 1873. And it had issues. My brothers had done a great job of keeping up with the necessary maintenance, but once I bought the duplex, the maintenance was on me. And it needed a lot of it over the years I owned it.

The attention it needed was an added level of stress on top of learning a new job, struggling to fit in with the culture there, and continuing to carry the baggage of unfinished business from all the previous traumas I was unconsciously dragging with me. It was like carrying a backpack full of rocks. With each new stressful event, including the demands of the home, I was putting another rock in the backpack, never offloading any of the weight, only adding to it. Eventually the bag would tear open.

Shortly after moving back to Eau Claire, I learned that the prostate cancer Dad had been diagnosed with years earlier and which had been treated was now out of remission. What little information I got from him indicated that he was still fighting.

With the return of Dad's cancer, I began thinking about my own medical history and what ran in my family. I still didn't have an answer to who my biological father was. Dad had a history of cancer. Bill Armson was overweight and had both diabetes and heart disease. When I went for my annual work physical, I was always asked about my family history of diseases. I had no way of answering the questions. I knew my family medical history on my mother's side, but because I didn't even know for sure who my father was, I couldn't answer about that side.

I decided it was time to get answers to the lingering question of who my father was. It had been nine years since I had last asked Mom about it. I contacted my Mom and told her I needed to talk with her. When I picked her up, we drove out to the airport on the edge of town. It was a quiet place where we would have no interruptions.

She admitted that what my father had said nine years earlier was true. Bill Armson was my biological father. That night, she shared many of the salacious details. When we got back to her house, Bill was sitting at the kitchen table. I told him that I knew the truth: that he was my father.

He cried. He said he wanted his other five boys to know who I was. I told him he would need to tell them if he wanted them to know because it wasn't my job to do that. He assured me he would. For the first time, I felt I had been seen and claimed. The secret of my paternity was finally out in the light, and I was relieved.

I hoped that Bill's acknowledgment would be the beginning of a new relationship with him.

12

In my effort to create stability in our life together, Jennifer and I decided to get married. I proposed to her while we were on a trip with my brothers to the Florida Keys. It was a special trip. I believed I had found my soulmate. We were passionate partners and lovers, but I had not done any of the work to heal my past traumas and internal wounding, so on a regular basis, there were triggers I wasn't aware of being activated.

Our arguments were intense, and I feared I was going to be abandoned again. I felt I wasn't enough. When I felt attacked, I got defensive, sarcastic, and passive aggressive, essentially dumping gasoline on a quickly growing inferno. I was never abusive, but I was certainly childish.

Boundaries were common fodder for tension between us. Jennifer struggled to set them with her son. I would try to set them from my tenuous position as a stepparent, but it was never received well by Owen. I was seldom supported by Jennifer and was often overruled by her in front of him. The older Owen got, the worse the trouble became.

Jennifer tried to enforce her requests, but he pushed with increasing force until his mother caved in and relented. I begged her not to do that. I was forbidden to hold him accountable for his actions, and his mother wouldn't hold him accountable. He wore her down, and it was exhausting for her. She'd tell him no and he would push, become belligerent, yell, and push some more until Jennifer couldn't take it anymore. Then she would kick him out of the house, which was what he wanted in the first place. He'd learned that he could use intimidation and the threat of violence to get his way.

I felt he needed to learn that his actions had consequences and that our home was the best place for him to learn that. She fought me. During one argument with Jennifer, I said that *someone* was going to hold Owen accountable for his actions, and it would either be us or the court system.

When I asked Owen to either do something or not do something, he came at me aggressively with his fist cocked back as if he were going to hit me. I stood my ground and said that he might be big enough to get away with that someday, but *this* wasn't that day. I become the enemy not only in Owen's eyes, but also in the eyes of his mother. And they became my enemies. It was no way to salvage a marriage.

I was halfway through my twenty-four-hour shift at the fire department when I received the call from Jennifer. Owen had been arrested. He was now fifteen. Four girls from school had accused him of sexual assault.

I immediately thought of Nicole. Had Owen harmed her too? I called her and was stunned and horrified by what she said about what had happened between her and her stepbrother. She said there was some consensual contact, and when she asked him to stop, he refused. When she tried to leave his bedroom following the assault, he blocked the door with his body and told her that if she told anyone what happened, he would kill me.

Tears immediately began to flow. My daughter had been assaulted in my own home. I had failed to protect her. I was speechless, but my inability to speak turned to an inner rage I was terrified was going to erupt in violence.

I left work, but I couldn't go home because I was afraid I'd kill Owen. I was as angry at myself as I was at him, and I was angry at my wife for not allowing me to discipline Owen for so many years. Owen had learned from the most influential woman in his life that no didn't mean no. I picked up Nicole at her grandparents' house and drove to the bowling alley where her mother, Paula, was bowling on a league to tell her what had happened.

After I talked with Paula, I went to the home of a friend and spent the night. In the morning I returned home to find Owen gone. Jennifer had whisked him away to his father's house the previous night.

Owen stayed with his father, Wade, for several weeks. Wade had never been a good role model, but Owen adored him. Wade had done time in prison for burglary, and after Owen was born, Jennifer knew she needed to get away from him. She did her best to protect Owen while not interfering with Wade's relationship with him.

After several weeks, Jennifer told me she needed to bring Owen home. I knew she was right, and I knew he couldn't be in the house with me or my daughters. I contacted Danielle's mother, Amanda, and told her what had happened to Nicole because I feared Danielle might have been assaulted too. In turn, Amanda contacted the Columbia County Sheriff's Department to interview Danielle. It was determined that Owen had not assaulted her.

Through all of this, I failed to call the police and tell them about Owen's assault on Nicole. Maybe I thought Amanda had already told them or that Paula would call them. Maybe I thought the Columbia County Sheriff's Department would contact the Eau Claire Police Department. Whatever I was thinking consciously, something else was happening beneath the surface of my conscious thought. Unconsciously, a fuse had been lit within me. I had been unable to protect myself all those years ago when I'd been assaulted, and now my own child had experienced something similar. She was about the same age when Owen assaulted her as I was when Ted assaulted me. My world closed in. I felt violated, exposed, and victimized all over again. Inside I was a child again, and I dealt with Nicole's horrible situation like the wounded child I was. I emotionally retreated inward.

Because of that, I didn't do what was best for my daughter. I wasn't her advocate or her champion. All I could think about was how I was feeling and what was happening to my marriage. I felt betrayed by Jennifer, and not only did I feel betrayed by Owen, I felt rage toward him.

"We can get through this," Jennifer insisted. "Other families have!"

"If Owen assaults Danielle too, how do I look at her and tell her I had the chance to keep her safe and chose not to?" I replied.

Jennifer found an apartment not far from our house and moved there with her son, taking much of our furniture with her because I told her she could have anything she wanted. I didn't want any arguments during her move. What was once our bedroom now contained only a dresser. The living room was completely empty and the majority of the kitchen cupboards were nearly empty. My world was being stripped bare right before my eyes, and I was too defeated to stop it.

Jennifer and I tried to maintain a friendship during our separation and toyed with the idea of repairing our broken marriage. For a time, our relationship felt new and exciting again. We laughed and were friends again. But the river of reality flowing beneath the unicorns and rainbows was the truth that there was an enormous amount of history that neither of us was capable of dealing with.

It didn't take long before our relationship blew up for the last time. I did what I'd always done: I looked for comfort where I could find it. I had a one-time transgression with another woman, and Jennifer found out. That only kept the misguided attempt to stay together from continuing even longer than it should have. There was no repairing the relationship with the mother after her son violated my daughter.

I wasn't aware of how any of Owen's court proceedings went. I only knew the outcome. He was sentenced to two years in a juvenile detention center. His punishment was only two years because he would then be eighteen years old, and his release would be mandatory at that time.

There was no justice for my daughter. Law enforcement hadn't been notified of the assault on her. She never got her day in court. She never got resolution.

13

It wasn't long after Jennifer left that I found myself in another relationship. I wasn't ready. I wasn't healthy. It was too soon and I was following a very old and very familiar pattern. I didn't stay single long enough to figure out who I was. I failed to spend the time I needed to heal from all that had just occurred, and I failed to give my daughter the support she needed. She and I needed to grieve and heal.

But I was alone and didn't want to be.

Paramedics and nurses staffed the medical helicopter based in Eau Claire. The aeromedical service hadn't been in town long. It was a new service the largest hospital in the region was now offering. I thought the brave souls who staffed the helicopter walked on water. All of us in emergency services got called out to traumas, but the helicopter was called to the worst of the worst. They were called when a few extra minutes saved could save a life. They were highly trained and highly skilled, and they had to be confident because lives depended upon it.

Brenda caught my attention one afternoon in the emergency room as she discussed an upcoming softball game with my partner on the ambulance. We had just transported a patient to the ER and I was getting my paperwork together from an ambulance call. I didn't play softball, but I was interested in the sport that day, and it wasn't because I had a newfound love of the game.

Brenda was an independent woman who had ambition and was solid in her career as a registered ER nurse and a flight nurse on the helicopter. She had her own money, and by all appearances, she was very different than Jennifer. Brenda didn't have children, which was incredibly appealing based on what I had just been through with my stepson. She owned her own home and had a close relationship with her parents, who lived across the river in Minnesota. We shared a love of the outdoors and both of us loved to camp and hike. Brenda was ten years older than me, and I saw her as a good role model for my daughters. On top of everything else, her smile and laugh were infectious. She seemed like a potentially great partner, and I couldn't help but be attracted to her.

My dad had been battling prostate cancer for many years, and by the summer of 1998, he was losing the battle. He was living north of Milwaukee, Wisconsin, and I traveled to see him whenever I could because we had grown closer over the years.

I had always left the emotional door open to my dad. I appreciated all he had done for me and realized he'd done what he could to the best of his ability. I would hug him and tell him I loved him when he still didn't know what to do with emotion. But by the end of his life, his face would genuinely light up when I arrived at his home, and he was able to say "I love you" when I left. I was moved and grateful that our relationship had deepened to that level.

Brenda had never met my dad, but my ex-wife, Jennifer, had known him for almost a decade. So when Jennifer asked if she could ride with me the next time I traveled to see my dad, I reluctantly agreed.

I knew being confined in a vehicle for several hours would be uncomfortable for several reasons, largely based on how our relationship had ultimately disintegrated. But I couldn't come up with a valid reason to say no. She had known my father for years, and it would have felt vindictive to refuse her the ride. He lived several hours away from Eau Claire, and it didn't make sense to tell Jennifer she had to drive herself there. I knew my dad was going to die soon and it could be the last time Jennifer saw him. I also didn't want more conflict, for any reason.

Wanting to avoid conflict was also one of the reasons I didn't tell Brenda that Jennifer had asked to ride with me. I knew she'd be angry, and I didn't want to deal with it. I also justified not telling her by reminding myself that our relationship was too new for any expectation that I would share all the details of my life.

The trip down was tense and uncomfortable. It was difficult to find topics we could easily discuss. When we arrived at Dad's home, Barb, Dad's wife, met us at the door. Dad was in bed and unresponsive.

The last time I'd been there, a few weeks earlier, he had been in his recliner in the living room. I had taken to bringing a radio with me so I could play music for Dad while I was there. I would put in a CD and see if he had some kind of physical response. I knew I'd made a good selection when I saw his feet moving back and forth to the beat of the music. Dad loved music.

This trip, Dad was not able to be in his chair. Barb, Jennifer, and I entered his bedroom. Jennifer said hello, Barb stepped out, and after a minute or two, Jennifer stepped out as I set up the CD player. I picked out an Enya CD that he'd seemed to enjoy the last time I visited, sat on the edge of the bed, and held his hand as we listened.

I couldn't help but think about where our relationship had been as I was growing up and how far it had come. He was not my father by blood, but he'd tried to be my father. And even though he often failed, he continued to show up as best he could. As time passed, we'd both softened. The sharp edges of our painful history faded, and we could now hug, smile, and laugh together. His breath slowed. I whispered, "I love you." Then he drew his last breath and slipped through the veil.

At first, I was numb. I studied the contours of his now lifeless face, memorizing the lines around his closed eyes, the evidence of a life lived. My tears began to flow and my stomach heaved as I tried to hold in the wail I knew was forcing its way out. I called for Barb and touched my father's hand one last time. Through tears, I whispered in his ear, "Goodbye."

I held myself together long enough to call my brothers and sister to tell them Dad was gone. When I went back to the living room, I wailed, no longer able to contain my sorrow. I sat in my father's chair, with my head on my knees and cried, my arms covering my head. Sounds I didn't recognize came from places within me I didn't know existed.

I didn't want to see the funeral director put my father's body in the black, impersonal body bag, so I waited in the living room. I looked up as he was wheeled past me. Never again would we laugh together. Never again would he want to teach me something. Never again would we sing together. Never again.

I watched from the second-story deck that overlooked the parking lot as the funeral director pushed the gurney toward the vehicle. The body bag was unzipped just enough to reveal my father's lifeless face. That was my final look at his physical form.

The trip back to Eau Claire was quiet. I cried. I was in a state of disbelief. The death of my father didn't seem real. It didn't seem possible he was gone. I dropped Jennifer off at her house and called Brenda from a nearby payphone and asked her if I could come over. I wanted support and I needed comfort.

It was late when I arrived and we went to bed. Brenda knew where Jennifer lived and knew what payphone I'd called from. She asked if Jennifer had gone with me to visit my dad, and I told the truth. "Yes, she did."

"Get out," Brenda replied. No further questions and no discussion. Just the demand that I leave.

It was representative of my turbulent relationship with Brenda. She was bright and smiling one minute and angry the next. I didn't know how to stay in the relationship, but I also didn't know how to leave. My fear of being alone overshadowed the realization that we had problems and no understanding of how to solve them.

We were still living in separate houses, and I was getting tired of living in the city. I told Brenda that I wanted to move to the country, away from people. I wanted some privacy and I wanted to get a horse. Brenda had grown up with horses and wasn't interested in having a horse again, but I'd grown up in the city and had always wanted a horse.

Neither of us suggested that we combine households. It was inferred. It wasn't a deliberate decision, it just happened. We began talking about getting a place with five acres, but before we even looked at our first place, we'd raised that to nothing less than twenty acres. And when we started looking, we quickly realized how small twenty acres was. It wouldn't afford us the privacy we both wanted.

We found a forty-acre piece of property south of town that we both liked. It had an old barn and a very old house that someone had tried to renovate. The property had enough open space for pastures and a hill we could climb that overlooked the beautiful countryside. Unlike the city, it was quiet and peaceful.

We looked at that place multiple times and decided to put in an offer. It was a low offer because we didn't see any value in the house itself and felt we would need to tear it down and start over. Our offer was rejected. We counter-offered and were rejected again.

We continued to drive out to the property to assess how much we wanted to invest in it. After a number of rejections and counteroffers, the price was still more than we could pay considering that we would have to tear down the house and build a new one. If we paid their asking price, we'd be stuck with the house, unable to tear it down and rebuild. After six months of attempting to strike a deal and dreaming about what our lives would be like to live in the country, we let the place go. The price was just too high.

For a while following that experience, I didn't want to look at properties. I needed a break. I found it difficult to get my hopes up about finding our dream property only to have the opportunity snatched away. It was a roller coaster I needed to get off of for a while.

After a short break from our intense search, we were driving back from a hike in the county forest when we saw a sign offering eighty acres for sale. We stopped. The gravel driveway was lined with large oak trees, and the grass between the oaks was mowed in a way that was both inviting and trance like. We had to see more. A slight rise in the terrain prevented us from seeing the house from the road. That suited us because it meant the place had the privacy we desperately wanted. We called our real estate agent while parked at the end of the driveway.

We were able to see the house and property that day. As we approached the house, we saw that it was a ranch style with a tuck under garage on the front. The house was almost completely surrounded by trees and was on a small hill that overlooked two small ponds. The eighty acres consisted of two, forty-acre parcels adjacent to five thousand acres of county forest land. The property was magnificent. The house, on the other hand, was a far cry from magnificent.

The house was a manufactured home that I thought was closer to the likes of a double-wide trailer that had been set high upon a basement. Said basement had clearly been constructed by the previous owner, who had no construction knowledge whatsoever.

The house had problems, but we felt it was livable, and some of the issues could be fixed. We loved the property and the wildlife that lived on it. We put in an offer, and it was accepted. I was being given the opportunity to learn that sometimes when I tried too hard to get what I thought was the right thing—in this case, the house we'd tried for six months to get—the Universe couldn't give me what was actually the right thing until I stopped trying so hard. Once I'd given up on that property, the Universe had dropped this beautiful eighty-acre property in our laps.

Both of our houses in the city sold quickly, and before we knew it, we were packing and beginning the move to the new property. I thought the move would make or break our relationship.

One of the subtle shifts that had occurred during our relationship, which had endured five years at that point, was the power dynamic. Brenda held more power in the relationship than me, and it had been established through anger. When something didn't go Brenda's way, she was angry. I didn't want to anger her, so I did my best to calm her while building resentment that I kept to myself.

The move represented that pattern. Near the end of our move and the combining of our households, my older sister came to our new house. "Is anything in this house yours?" she asked when she and I were alone in the living room for a moment.

As I looked around the room and thought about my reply, I realized something. There was very little in the house that was mine, and that was the case because I didn't want to annoy Brenda. To make peace, I let her furnish the house as she desired. I didn't know how to resolve conflict without surrendering. The house was filled and decorated with all of Brenda's things, from the art on the walls and the furniture right down to the dishes. My things were either in the basement or out in the garage.

I'd had the same pattern with Jennifer. I'd given in to her desires instead of rocking the boat. In both cases, I tried to keep the peace to avoid their anger and avoid risking an end to the relationship. I was terrified of leaving relationships and terrified of being abandoned. More than anything, I was terrified of being alone.

At a subconscious level, I believed I needed to be acquiescent or people would leave me.

14

I'd dreamt of having my own horse since I was a child. Some of my earliest memories were of horses and the relationship between horse and human, and I longed for that relationship in my own life. I wanted connection. In the old Westerns, the cowboys loved their horses, and their horses were loyal, trusted partners with the cowboys. The horse came running to save the cowboy trapped on the roof of a building as the bad guys closed in, and the daring cowboy would leap from the rooftop, landing on the back of his trusty steed. Then he and his horse would make their jubilant escape together. They were a team.

The time had finally arrived. I was financially stable enough to afford a horse. I lived on eighty acres, so I had enough room. There was one glaring problem: I didn't know anything about owning a horse. I had ridden horses at a riding stable or ones that were owned by friends, but I had no idea how to keep one alive myself. I needed help.

That help came from Denise. Denise was from Madison, Wisconsin, and had recently been hired on at our fire department. She had horses, and she boarded them at Fred's farm. Fred was a crusty, sharp-tongued, old-school battalion chief in our department. At home and away from work, Fred was a very different man. He was a kind man who loved his wife and the animals that lived with him on his beautiful property.

When I learned that Denise had horses, had worked as a wrangler out West, and was willing to let me play with her horses, we were instantly friends. She was willing to share her knowledge about horses with anyone who asked, and she invited me to Fred's to ride.

Denise was happy to have Brenda join us, and Brenda did join us once, but I noticed that Brenda got angry when I asked her if she wanted to come ride. Brenda had grown up with horses, and I thought she would enjoy some time in the saddle. I wanted to ride, and I didn't want any awkwardness about my going riding with another woman. I had nothing to hide.

Brenda and Denise knew each other from work. When Denise came to our department, we weren't sure of her sexual orientation. That's why it came as such a surprise to me when Brenda exclaimed in an argument that she wasn't comfortable with me hanging out with Denise and didn't think it was appropriate.

In my confusion and frustration, I bellowed, "I don't think she even likes men!"

It didn't matter to Brenda. She was going to be mad. I backed away from riding horses with Denise because I wanted to keep the peace. But I knew Denise could and would help me find my first horse. I trusted her as a friend, and more importantly, she had the day-to-day horse knowledge I lacked. I asked her if she would help me find my first equine partner, and she said she was excited to help.

It didn't take long for her to find a five-year-old Appaloosa gelding named Royale at a local riding and boarding facility. Royale had been a trail horse and was advertised as "bomb proof," meaning he was as solid as he could be. I met Denise at the facility to meet what was to become my first horse.

He was a chestnut brown, tall, thin horse with a beautiful gray main and tail. He wasn't particularly engaging or interested, but he wasn't disinterested either. We brought him into the indoor arena, and he followed me as I walked around the arena, just like I'd seen in the horse training videos I watched on RFD-TV. I thought that had to be a good thing. When I saddled him and climbed on, he didn't buck me off. I saw that as another great indication that it was meant to be.

I bought him. I didn't negotiate the price and I didn't get a veterinarian prepurchase checkup. I was impatient. I had my first horse, and I was too excited to do any of the things an experienced horse person would have done.

I boarded him at the facility while I learned the ins and outs of what I needed to do to keep him alive. At home, I needed to create a space for him to live. Brenda and I had eighty acres, but the land was almost completely wooded. Brenda agreed to let me clear a very small space, maybe a quarter of an acre, for him to live on.

I was eager to learn more about what it meant to be a horseman, and I knew I had a lot to learn. I had been watching as many of the RFD-TV horse clinicians as I could. How they approached their horses was important to me, and only a couple of them resonated with me. Some only viewed the horse as a tool and treated them as such. Some were too heavy-handed and didn't give the horse the respect I felt they deserved.

I was given two free tickets to a live event that one of my favorite clinicians was conducting. We drove to the event, and when we walked into the arena, I heard music playing and saw several people playing with their horses. With no ropes or halters, the horses stayed with their humans. It looked like they were dancing. The people playing were not the clinicians. They looked like normal people—like me. It was exciting.

Throughout the course of the weekend, I watched, listened, and learned. I learned how horses' minds worked. I learned what was important to them and what wasn't important to them. Clearly, the system that clinician was selling worked. The real question I had to answer for myself was, could I make it work for me and my new equine partner?

I wanted the kind of relationship with my horse I saw demonstrated. I wanted a deeply connected, nonjudgmental relationship *somewhere* in my life, and deep within, I knew I wanted it with a horse.

But I doubted my own ability. A woman was working the stand that was selling the entry-level kit containing some DVDs and equipment. After several conversations with her, I decided to buy the kit, which cost several hundred dollars, and begin my horsemanship journey.

I watched the DVDs. When I went to the boarding facility to see my horse, I began practicing what I had previously seen on TV. But I had no idea what I was doing, and my poor horse had no idea what I was *trying* to do. We were both confused and frustrated. Being able to spend only a limited amount of time with Royale made for slow progress.

I knew I wanted him at home with me so I could spend more consistent time with him, so I needed to create a safe place for him there. Cutting down trees was going to be a difficult thing for Brenda to watch. During the planning stages of which trees would be felled and which would stay, Brenda tied orange ribbons around the trees she wanted to keep. I agreed to save those trees. I felt they would create great shade in the pasture. Like Brenda, I struggled with cutting down live, healthy trees, but I wanted to share my home with my new partner. And it was important for him to have a safe home.

I solicited help from some coworkers to take down the trees. The day we began clearing the small plot of land, Brenda decided she couldn't be there to watch. My friends thought it would be funny to move one of the ribbons indicating that tree shouldn't be taken down. I panicked and began yelling at them for cutting the wrong tree. I completely overreacted, and they thought it was hilarious that I did. All I could hear in my mind was how angry Brenda was going to be and the hell I would catch for the error.

Without any urging from me, Brenda decided to get a horse too. She'd grown up having a horse and fondly told the story of her dad coming home with one. She also talked about her and her sister playing with the horse, but I didn't think she'd loved the experience of owning and caring for it. So I was pleasantly surprised when she said she wanted to get a horse too. Soon we had two horses.

After a year of traveling forty-five minutes each way to and from the boarding stable, we were able to bring our horses home. I loved the fact that I would be able to see them every day and practice the things I was learning from the DVDs.

I found solace and comfort when I was with the horses. The world didn't feel so hectic when I was with them. Time stood still and stress melted away. The turmoil of the previous day's emergency calls was silenced by the breeze flowing through leaves in the trees. I focused my attention on the body language of my horse. Touching him with my heart put me back in my body and out of my head, where all my anxiety lived. It was sacred time, and I could rest emotionally.

As I found peace with Royale, my relationship with Brenda deteriorated. On top of all her previous frustrations, she was now angry about us having horses, despite the fact that she had gotten one herself and agreed to bring them home. If I needed to be gone for work, she insisted I find people to look in on the horses and feed them, even if she was home. She wanted nothing to do with them.

I was feeling more trapped with each passing day. Each new argument pushed me further and further away from her. She seemed to be mad at everything. There were other changes between us as well. What once was a vibrant and exciting sex life began to dwindle. Several times a week turned into a few times a month. In time, that turned into once every few months. I asked her about it. I wanted to understand and do something about it.

"It's not you, it's me. I just don't feel like it," she said.

I was doing everything I could to be understanding. I researched what might be happening with her physically so I could better understand what she was going through. "I'm still here and I still want intimacy to be a part of our relationship," I pleaded.

But it didn't improve. I slowly resigned myself to the sad and lonely fact that sex and intimacy might never again be a part of my life. I didn't want to live like that.

Because I was not in a healthy place emotionally, I viewed her lack of interest as a statement about me. Physical intimacy with her was a way of proving to myself that I was okay. In other words, if a woman was willing to share that most sacred of acts with me, willing to be that vulnerable with me, I must be okay. And even though Brenda was telling me her lack of interest in sex wasn't because of me,

I still felt there must be something wrong with me. Clearly, I was no longer desirable. I wasn't enough.

Her anger continued. She hated her job. Some days, it appeared she hated everything. She came home after work and spent the better part of the evening complaining about her day. I tried to be supportive and allow her the space to vent, but listening to her negativity was emotionally draining. And while I did my best to redirect her attention to anything positive in her day, that strategy seldom worked.

She complained daily about her job at the hospital, while she often reminisced about how much she missed working at a larger hospital in Minneapolis, Minnesota, and how much she loved working there. She felt important and needed there. I wanted to find a solution for her. I wanted her life to be more peaceful, which would make *my* life more peaceful. I wanted a return to the relationship we had started with. Life back then was fun, adventurous, and full of laughter. I wanted that again. I wanted to rescue our relationship.

Unfortunately, I would soon be on the receiving end of a rescue.

15

Following the tragic events of September 11, 2001, there was a resurgence of interest in the fire service and the important role first responders played in the defense and safety of our country's citizens. After that horrific day, the fire department in Eau Claire was given the distinction of being an urban search and rescue team for the State of Wisconsin. I was a member of that team. We specialized in collapse rescue, confined space rescue, trench rescue, and high angle rescue. We had very technical and intensive training in all these disciplines.

Another role I filled in my job was that of a search and recovery SCUBA diver. I had gotten my original Open Water Diver Certification before I was hired in Eau Claire. I knew they had a dive team, and I thought it would make me more hirable. After I arrived in Eau Claire and was put on the dive team, I received the remainder of my certifications, which included Rescue Diver, Advanced Open Water Diver, and Ice Diver.

All were dangerous. As risk management expert Gordon Graham says, low frequency, high risk activities were the most dangerous assignments we in the fire service could do. Because we didn't have those assignments often, we weren't as proficient as we would have been if we'd had them often. When we did dive, it was very dangerous. Only a few times in my fifteen years as a diver did I recover bodies from beneath the ice. If we trained on ice diving procedures, it was once a year. Cutting a small hole in the ice and then swimming one hundred feet away from that hole is dangerous by anyone's standards.

On the afternoon of December 18, 2007, I was scheduled for our ice dive training. At roughly four in the afternoon, I slipped through the small hole in the ice and into the cold, dimly lit silence of the lake. I could hear my breath pass through my regulator when I inhaled, I could hear my bubbles when I exhaled, and I could see the bubbles leave and slowly rise to the surface only to find their escape cut short by the thick layer of ice overhead. They couldn't escape—and neither could I if something went wrong.

Nighttime temperatures had been below zero in early December, which was great for making ice. Lakes in the area were already frozen over with more than enough ice to walk on and certainly enough to conduct our annual ice diving training for the fire department.

By then, I had been a search and recovery diver for a career fire department for more than a decade. It wasn't my first rodeo, but because of the danger involved, I never took diving under the ice for granted.

To gain entry to the water, a triangular hole was cut with a chain saw through the ice, roughly four feet on each side. That hole was the only way in or out of the ice-cold water. Unlike recreational diving, where they teach to dive with a buddy, public safety diving is conducted alone. There was no one in the water with me. At the surface, two people held my life in their hands.

Mark was my communications guy that day, and he wore a headset and a microphone. I had a speaker and microphone in my full-face diving mask, so Mark and I could talk freely. He gave me instructions if they were needed and informed me that when I was reaching the end of my safety line, I would be one hundred feet from my exit hole.

When I needed to conduct an underwater search, there were times when the darkness of the murky water closed in on me. The rhythmic sound of my breath and exhaled bubbles were a constant reminder to slow my breathing. I needed every bit of the air in my tank, especially if something went wrong.

At times it became lonely. I was alone with my thoughts and alone with my imagination. The visibility underwater could range from less than ten feet on a clear day to no visibility at all. During some dives, I could place my hand directly on my mask and not see it.

My imagination would begin the slow steady walk to an all-out run when I was searching for a dead body. I would see glimpses of an imaginary arm or a face just outside the veil of my visibility. When the murky water was particularly bad, I knew the only way I was going to find the deceased person was to run into them. Literally. That was the stuff nightmares were made of: face-to-face with a dead body with no warning.

To have a familiar and friendly voice on the other end of that communication line was a godsend when my imagination was getting the best of me. His voice could quell the rising anxiety that sometimes crept in. I wasn't alone.

Mark was a kind man with a huge heart and many years of service on the fire department. He had a slow, melodic rhythm to his voice. I had been assigned to Mark's crew in the firehouse more than once in my career. I learned a lot from him about being a paramedic because he was one of the first in the city to hold that license. I learned a lot about being an officer from him as well. I'd trusted Mark with my life many times before. I had a lot of respect for him, and I was glad he was on the other end of my communication link for that training dive.

Don was in charge of my lifeline to the surface. To this day, I don't know of anyone I worked with at the fire department who was more dedicated to the job or who demanded more excellence from himself and those with whom he worked. I always got along with him and had the utmost respect for him, his knowledge, and his dedication.

My lifeline was a rope that was marked off in ten-foot increments, up to a hundred feet. Don had one end of the line, and the other was clipped to my gear. If I were to become unconscious, I couldn't drop the line. But the line itself could prove deadly if it became entangled somewhere between me and Don.

Becoming entangled on underwater debris such as a tree or a long forgotten structure built during the heyday of the logging era could prove to be inescapable. The remnants of a bridge pier submerged for 150 years could end my life. There seemed to be no shortage of hazards to avoid or manage during a routine search and rescue dive.

My fellow divers and I accepted the risks, and we did our best to avoid getting into trouble. I was unafraid, but I was also aware. I trusted my gear, and I trusted my teammates.

The lifeline and the communication line ran together as they made their way through the dark water to me. Mark, Don, and those lines that bound us together through the unforgiving water were my only connection to the life-giving air above the thick ice.

I was the last diver to go down that day in December. Another diver had used the buoyancy control device (BCD) and tank I put on in the temporary shelter erected on the ice. I could feel the weight on my shoulders increase dramatically as I donned my gear.

Putting on the heavy gear to dive was always a chore. It was cumbersome on land, and the closer you got to being fully geared up, the harder it was to move and see. During training dives, I always had help getting dressed out. My helper also acted as another safety check. They were another set of eyes on my gear to help ensure nothing was broken and everything could perform safely. Placing my life in the hands of my fellow firefighters and my state-of-the-art gear was always an act of trust.

Diving under the ice was cold. The suit we used was called a dry suit. As the name implied, the intention was to keep the diver dry. Any wrinkle or fold around the neck seal meant that cold water would seep in and slowly begin to soak the clothing under the suit. By the time the diver knew it was happening, it was already too late. They were wet.

My dry suit protected me from the water, the cold, and any contaminants that might be in the water unless, of course, they leaked in. The suit was made of heavy rubber. It had feet, like kid's pajamas, and a hood made of a thin rubber that covered my head but not my face.

The last thing I did before leaving the tent was squat down, make myself as small as possible, and push as much air out of the suit as I could, holding the neck seal open to allow the excess air to escape. If there was too much air left in the suit when I went underwater, the pressure of the water on my suit would push the air bubble around in the suit. If my head was higher than my feet while underwater, the bubble of air could push my hood and mask off my face. If my feet were higher than my head, the air bubble would travel to my feet and cause an uncontrolled ascent to the surface that could prove fatal.

Not only was too much air left in the suit a problem, taking out too much air was also a problem. That would result in squeeze. Squeeze was a painful experience but not deadly. As the diver descended, the pressure on his body from the water increased, and all the creases in the suit, such as those at the elbows and the backs of the knees, would get squeezed, much like having your sock get wrinkled up in your shoe.

There was a valve in the suit on my left arm that gave me limited control to let excess air out of my suit while I was underwater. There was another valve on my chest I could push to put air into my suit if I needed it. It was a delicate balance.

The trek across the ice and snow to the ice hole was treacherous because the rubber boots that were part of my dry suit didn't have much traction. At the entrance hole, my helper had situated my BCD and tank behind me so I could put them on like an extremely heavy vest. The hoses were connected to my suit, I put on my full-face mask, and the head straps were secured in place behind my head.

I could freely talk to Mark through the communication system. Comms were good and Don was on my safety line. I had 2500 PSI of air, well above the 500 PSI minimum. It was more than enough air for a short training dive.

The small lake was home to small fish, ducks, and geese, and in the winter, it was a popular place for ice fishing. Ice fishing shacks dotted the frozen lake as well as folks all bundled up, braving the cold with no shelter at all, sitting on a bucket, hunched over their hole

Because of the people fishing, we did our best to place our entrance hole away from the ice fishing shacks. After all, we were creating a hole in the ice that would be unsafe until it refroze. The lake itself wasn't deep, maybe ten feet or so where we were diving. At the bottom was several more feet of silt, sediment, and muck that was so fine I couldn't feel it if I put my hand into it. If I disturbed the bottom sediment with a diving fin, all visibility was lost. It was like shaking a dirty snow globe. If I was very careful and moved very slowly and deliberately, I could keep the sediment disturbance to a minimum.

Looking down, I could see only darkness. Looking up, I could see the diffuse blue tint of sunlight passing through the thick ice.

One goal of the training dive was to get comfortable in my gear again. Another goal was to conduct a search pattern that consisted of ever-increasing concentric circles expanding away from my entrance hole. I would swim in a circle, and Don would let out more line when I had completed a circle.

During my dive, Mark asked me if a could see the wheel—a pattern that had been shoveled in the snow on the surface of the ice. Sunlight shone more easily through the shoveled area. The wheel was a safety measure for the unlikely event that my safety/comms line became detached from me. I could look up and see the wheel. Spokes on the wheel pointed toward my exit hole.

When I looked up through the murky water, I did in fact see the wheel and the spokes. I informed Mark that I could see them and overheard Don inform Mark that I was eighty feet out. In other words, I was eighty feet from my exit. Eighty feet from life-giving air.

When I looked up and answered Mark, my head was above my feet. I heard small bubbles escaping my tank. The sound was coming from behind my head. My mask began slowly pushing off my face, and I could feel my hood coming off my head. I held my mask on my face with one hand and dove down in an attempt to move the ever-expanding air bubble out of my head and face. Exhaling as I spoke, I told Mark, "I think I have a small leak." Those were the last words I said to Mark.

At that moment, I heard a loud crack, the explosion muffled by the water. I didn't feel the massive rush of air that hit my face as it ripped my hood and mask off. I did, however, feel the immediate sensation of the freezing water stinging my face and head. I could no longer see clearly, just blurry movement, as if petroleum jelly were over my eyes. My mask and hood were gone. My communications were gone. My air was gone. I couldn't tell Mark that something had gone horribly wrong. I had no way of telling him I was in serious trouble. I couldn't tell him I needed help.

Panic quickly began to overtake me. I couldn't breathe. While holding my breath, I had floated up, and my head and shoulder struck the underside of the ice. I felt the inescapable solidity of the ice and saw the sunlight. Air and survival were that close. Twelve inches of ice separated me from life. I was in a tomb.

I believed no one knew I was in trouble. Panic gripped my chest as it burned with the desire to breathe. I knew I couldn't hold my breath much longer. I was going to have to inhale. I was terrified. I searched for my backup regulator, sweeping my arm for it, but found nothing. My head hit the ice again and my chest burned deeper. I again searched for my backup regulator and again found nothing. My head again hit the ice. I had to inhale. I had to breathe. I had no choice. So this is where it's going to end, I thought. I made one more sweep for my backup regulator, found it, put it in my mouth, and inhaled.

But there was no air to inhale. Nothing. It was like breathing into a plastic bag held tightly over my face.

Everything stopped. There was silence. The profound loneliness and dread I had been experiencing had been replaced with overwhelming peace. Peace like I had never known. A peace that swept away the last fragments of panic. Tranquil darkness had descended upon the recesses of my soul. All the betrayal and pain that had been a large part of my human experience were gone. Calm had replaced chaos. As I faded into unconsciousness, the world and my life began to slip away, and my vision faded to black.

Then I was sitting on the ice, screaming. My gear was being ripped off me. People were in my face, yelling to get my attention, attempting to calm me. Chaos and confusion had returned. What was happening? Where was I?

Coworkers were in my face. Questions came at me in rapid succession. I wasn't following. I couldn't understand. Off in the distance, I could hear someone screaming. Eventually I realized it was me.

Don had pulled me out. Mark and Don had saved my life. Mark had heard my comment about the leak, but after that, he heard only noise, like a constant roar. He tried a few times to talk to me, and when I didn't answer, he told Don to pull me in. As Don pulled me in, the sensation on the safety line was that of having a fish on the line. The line jumped and tugged chaotically. He could feel the panic in the line. Crew members on the surface yelled at Don to pull me in faster. Don said he didn't want to pull the regulator from me if I was trying to get it. He pulled me in slowly, steadily, and deliberately.

I was unconscious and not breathing when I got to the hole. My face was beet red and my eyes were wide open. The backup regulator was in my mouth. They quickly stripped the gear from me to start CPR. "It was like you woke up," Don later said about what happened when he took the regulator out of my mouth.

Someone had called my girlfriend to come pick me up at the lake. Brenda was a competent helicopter flight nurse with years of experience. I trusted her medical judgment. As we were driving back to my fire station to get my gear, my throat began to close. When I talked, it sounded like I was talking through water, and it was becoming harder to breathe. My airway was closing. Once again, fear began to grip my chest. Brenda immediately turned around and drove me to the local hospital emergency department. After exams, tests, procedures, and time, the swelling in my throat subsided and we headed back to the station to gather my clothes and head home.

A reporter from a local TV station was on the ice at our training session the day of my accident, filming a story to be aired that evening. The girlfriend of a friend of mine who was also a firefighter worked at the news station, and the cameraman told her what had happened. Because I was the last diver that day, the reporter had packed up his equipment and was walking off the ice when the commotion about my drowning started. He wasn't filming. When he turned back to see what was happening, he realized it was bad and chose not to film it.

When I heard about his decision, I was incredibly grateful because the story and film footage would have aired on the evening news—the day before my mother's birthday. As a faithful watcher of the news, she would have been watching.

My mother was a sweet woman who suffered with her own inner demons, and she loved me. She once told me that she cried every time she heard a siren from an emergency vehicle. When I asked her why, she said, "Because someone is having a really bad day, and I'm afraid for your safety."

She cried when she watched the news, which she faithfully did every evening. She cried because bad things happened in the world and people were cruel to each other. She also knew my job was dangerous. I kept some things about my job from her because I didn't want her to worry. Even so, she saw some events in the newspaper and knew I'd been there.

For years, and well into her advancing dementia, she marked my workdays on her calendar. That was no easy task because my workdays varied. I was often on one day and off the next. She couldn't remember my dog's name, but she knew my work schedule. She knew I was working the day before her birthday, and she knew I was a search and recovery diver.

Thankfully, the reporter's decision saved my mother from a level of grief that would have destroyed her.

16

My world felt tight and unfamiliar, and I felt lost and alone. One moment melted into another, and it was difficult to either move or think. It was as if I were still underwater. Sadness and terror were persistently near the surface, waiting to spill onto those around me

Seeing anything that resembled panic on TV sent me into a full-on panic attack. A story of cows caught in a flood showed one flailing, trying not to drown. Without realizing it, I fled the room. When I realized where I was, I found myself in a spare bedroom, unable to breathe. A scream rose from within, but I contained it because I was embarrassed. Brenda didn't understand what was happening with me and I had no way of explaining it. Hell, I didn't know what was going on with me.

We argued. Everything I trusted seemed to be eroding beneath my feet. Our relationship was not in the best place before the accident and wasn't helped by it.

Two days after the accident, which happened the week before Christmas, Brenda left for her parents' home in Minnesota. I spent the following day at home alone with my tortured visions and memories of what had happened, vomiting most of the day. I felt as alone as I'd been under the ice. The one person I had hoped would support me had left.

Then calls from my bosses at work began to come in.

"Hey, Rob, I heard what happened. Glad you're okay. You coming to work on Sunday?"

"I thought I would make that decision on Saturday," I replied, frustrated that I was being pushed to return. I knew they needed to fill my place if I wasn't coming in, but by contract, I had until the day before my shift to inform them if I was going to be in. It was the holidays, and if I didn't go in to work, some younger firefighter was either going to get the opportunity for some overtime or they were going to be ordered to work and get the overtime whether they wanted it or not.

"Well, let us know as soon as possible."

Getting my shift filled seemed more important than how I was doing.

By December 21, I couldn't stay at home alone any longer. I went to Minnesota to be with Brenda and her family. The air was still tense between Brenda and me, but it was better than being alone. I again received a call from work, this time from a different boss.

"Hey Rob, I heard what happened. Glad you're okay. You going to be in to work on Sunday?"

I told him I would decide on Saturday.

"Well, let us know as soon as you can."

I could hear the frustration in his voice. I was interfering with his ability to get his job of filling the schedule completed. I felt pressured to return to work, but I felt incapable of making a decision.

I was wrestling with the significance of what had happened. I wanted to downplay the event. If my bosses felt I could return to duty, maybe I was making more out of it than was warranted. If I didn't return to work on Sunday, December 23, then a less senior firefighter was going to be ordered to work. I would ruin someone's Christmas.

When I received the call that Saturday asking if I was going to return to work the next day, I was on my way home from Minnesota. And I felt guilty. I didn't feel ready to return to work but I was okay enough to leave town. I heard the voice in my head say I was faking it to get attention, and I felt shame. I no longer trusted anything or anyone, including myself. I felt abandoned and betrayed by people, including those closest to me, and my equipment. I hadn't told anyone in my family what had happened, but Brenda knew. If the person with whom I was in my most significant relationship felt the event was so insignificant she could leave town immediately following it, then why should I feel it was big deal. I agreed to go to work on Sunday.

In the two weeks that followed, I was angry and afraid like I had never been before. Every tone that came into the station alerting us of a call sent my system into overdrive. It took everything I had to not completely shut down. I was terrified of being in a situation in which I might feel trapped. That included burning buildings because the walls often felt as if they were closing in when I was in one. Sometimes the walls actually *were* collapsing or the ceiling was coming down.

That was how my life felt: The walls were closing in, the ceiling was collapsing on top of me, and the floor was giving way. I had nothing to stand on and no one to rely on. I longed for death. I was frustrated that I had been saved. After the panic ceased, I had found peace in the solitude that lived under the ice. In those silent, suspended moments before I was ripped from my icy tomb, there was no question in my mind that I was going to die. And in that quiet darkness, I resigned myself to the fact that my life was ending right there, right then. When I was pulled from under the ice, I was returned to a world of chaos and confusion, fear and mistrust. My life was now worse than when I started my dive that day.

Memories, visions, and nightmares were constant. A smell could immediately send me into a panic attack. My only advocate was my personal physician, Dr. Reid, who had been my physician for years. I trusted him and felt he was the only one in my corner, the only one not judging me for the hot mess I was. I also knew I needed professional help because I was at risk of taking my own life to make the chaos stop. While I had thought about committing suicide many times before, this time I realized I might do it. A few weeks after the accident, I began seeing a therapist.

That first session with the therapist, my nerves were so frayed I could barely sit in the chair. Pacing and moving were a defense to the rising tide of anxiety. I wanted to run, and I realized there was no way to outrun the shit show that had suddenly become my life. There was no way to outrun myself. As painful as it was, I had to face this new chapter of my new life head-on.

The accident had happened without warning or choice. Being in that office, being vulnerable and asking for help, was my choice, and I knew it was the first step. I thought— or at least hoped—that I would finally begin to feel better. I was not prepared for what happened next.

"What did it feel like to be under the ice?" he asked in a flat, monotone voice.

The rest of the session was a blur. I felt nauseous when I left his office and stopped on the side of the road three times on my way home to open my car door and vomit.

Prior to that question, I hadn't remembered what it really felt like to be under the ice. I had no memory of the sensation of my head hitting the underside of the solid ice, no memories of details, and no conscious emotions attached to being entombed under the impenetrable ice. I knew I had been there, trapped, but I could not recall the actual sensations of it all. His question came without warning and felt like a sucker punch to the gut. It could almost have been someone else's terrifying story. But when he asked that question, I was instantly transported to where

I'd been under the ice, my head banging off of the cold, solid barrier. Panic gripped my chest just as tightly as it had on that fateful day.

The question initiated a cascade of terror. I felt there was nowhere to escape the sensation of my head against the ice. I was confined and trapped every hour of every day, everywhere I went. I felt as though I were standing in the middle of a crowded room and everyone had backed away from me. The room fell silent as I screamed, but no sounds were coming out of my mouth. Everyone in the room was staring at me with a look of disdain.

Unfortunately, I was left hanging by the therapist who opened that wound. My next appointment was canceled by his office and rescheduled. That appointment was also canceled and I was told that because they didn't know when the therapist would be back at work, they couldn't reschedule me. He was apparently on leave of some kind, and they didn't bother to assign another therapist to me.

I found another therapist on my own. During my first appointment with her, she said, "You're not still at work, are you?"

I told her I was.

"That's not a good idea," she said. "Because of your current mental state, if there's another critical incident, it could be career or life ending for you or someone on your crew."

"Then you're going to have to tell my boss," I replied.

She looked me right in the eye. "I'll do that," she said.

I was off on injury leave again, and I knew it wouldn't go down well with the brass.

I was awash in emotions, and Brenda had no idea what to do with me. I didn't know what to do with me either. Brenda and I had already grown apart, and the accident was like an immovable wedge between us.

I thought about ending my life many times in the first twelve months following the accident. I knew I was a mess, and I saw myself as a burden to everyone around me. Just as I hadn't been able to find a way out when I was trapped under the ice, I couldn't see a way out of the downward spiral I was in. And I wanted the kind of peace I'd found as I was losing consciousness while under the ice.

Brenda told me I was mean when I yelled at her. I yelled because I didn't feel heard or understood. She felt abandoned and unsupported, and she was right. I didn't have the capacity to be supportive. I had nothing to give. She wanted to know when I was going back to work. I didn't think I could ever go back to work. She wanted to know what I was planning on doing next with my life if I didn't go back to the fire department. I had no idea. I felt lost and without purpose. Perhaps worse, I felt hopeless because I often thought this was how my life would always be from that point on.

Her questions left me frustrated. "I have no idea what's happening!" I screeched. "I've never had an experience like this before!" Once again, I had yelled. I couldn't control my emotions, and I felt embarrassed and ashamed about it. Even so, her questions and her attitude toward me and my situation felt selfish.

Robert Goodland

My boss said, "What's the big deal, Rob?" He thought I was making a big deal out of *nothing*. He'd been there on the ice that day. He'd witnessed what had happened. Was I making a big deal out of nothing? Was I simply crying for attention? I tried to keep my erupting emotions contained and hidden from view so I would appear normal, like I had my shit together. But the truth was, inside, the razor-sharp fractured shards of my being were tearing me to shreds.

170

17

The closest thing to peace I could find was when my face was pressed against the warm winter coat of my horse. Sometimes I cried. Other times, I simply rested my head against him, listening to him eat. What was I going to do with my life?

I didn't know if I was ever going to be able to go back to work at the fire department. I knew I would never again be a search and rescue diver. And the thought of breathing through a mask, dependent upon the air on my back to keep me alive while fighting a fire, brought about chest-crushing anxiety. The only time I felt at peace was in the presence of a horse.

A month after the accident, I received a phone call from the corporate office of Parelli Natural Horsemanship, a program I had been studying through a DVD set I'd purchased. I was told I had won a two-week on-campus course. I didn't know I had entered a drawing when I purchased the DVDs, and I was speechless. The course was in Pagosa Springs, Colorado, and I was set to attend about eight months later, in September. I was going to be in the place where the master horseman I was watching on DVD had filmed all the shows, and I would be learning from him.

Winning that course started a slow-rolling cascade of beautiful events that forever changed my life. The most important jewel was that it put something in my future I was excited about. On a daily basis, I weighed the options for ending my life. Having that trip placed like a carrot out there in my future kept me alive.

The same month I won the course I also made the decision, once and for all, to quit smoking. I now knew what it felt like to drown. Being a paramedic, I knew that if I didn't quit, I would contract any number of lung diseases, some of which would cause fluid to build up in my lungs, giving me the sensation of drowning. Since I already knew what that felt like, I knew I would lie in my deathbed cursing myself for not quitting. It was a powerful motivation.

That September, Brenda and I went to the Parelli Campus in Pagosa Springs, Colorado, for the two-week course. She decided to come along and paid full price for her training. I didn't understand why. She appeared to hate the horses and everything they stood for.

I had not yet returned to work, and I knew I was going to have to make a decision soon to return or leave—whether or not I received disability retirement. The idea of leaving my career felt like jumping off a cliff. I made good money and had good benefits. The message I was receiving from Brenda was that she was not going to carry me financially until I got myself figured out.

Being in Colorado on the horse campus was thrilling. Seeing the very landscape I had been watching on the videos was fun, and meeting Pat Parelli, the founder of the program, and his wife, Linda, was like meeting a movie star.

I loved my two weeks on campus. I learned about horses at a level I had never known. But Brenda was angry, and we fought frequently. More than once, she stormed off while we were working on assignments. I felt emotionally torn. I didn't want her feeling frustrated, and yet, I wanted to learn for myself. To follow her and comfort her might have been good for her and ultimately better for our relationship in the short run, but it would have interrupted my opportunity to learn while I was there. I wanted my experience on campus to be as magical as possible, and I didn't know if I would ever have the opportunity to return. Brenda was not having a good experience. Her frustrations were clearly visible to me and everyone around us, and I found them frustrating and embarrassing.

When I left Colorado, I felt energized with the idea that maybe there was something I could do with my life that wasn't firefighting. A spark had been lit and was beginning to grow within me. Maybe I could make a living training horses and teaching people. For the first time in months,

I felt the emotion that had long ago left me and almost felt foreign: hope.

But my interest in a new career path that included horses was definitely not what Brenda had in mind. When I mentioned the idea of becoming an instructor instead of going back to the fire department, Brenda was furious. I didn't know if I had the capacity to return to the fire department and I was hurt and confused by her anger. I needed support, not rage. I felt trapped—by the prospect of my job killing me and by Brenda. If I followed my heart, I would suffer Brenda's wrath. But if I didn't follow my heart, I would be denying what was calling to me and giving me the first glimmers of hope I'd felt in a long time.

What little was left of our relationship continued to crumble. We were having the same argument over and over. She was mad about the same things. In frustration, I began to make my intentions known when we argued.

"We are not going to have this same argument in six months."

"What's that supposed to mean?" she asked.

"In six months, we will either have worked this out or I will have left. Either way, we will not be having this same argument."

Late that fall, I went back to work, but only during the day. The doctor my employer had sent me to had not wanted me to return to full duty yet. He recommended that I work half of my twenty-four-hour shift for a period of time before returning to full duty. I went to work during the day and returned home at night. It gave me an opportunity to ease back into the routine of work without compounding my trauma and delaying my healing with sleepless nights.

When it was time for me to return to full duty with no restrictions, my doctor, who had been so kind and compassionate to me, informed me that he was giving me a disability because of his diagnosis of post-traumatic stress disorder. I had no idea what that meant.

Within days, I was notified that I was required to see another city-appointed physician to evaluate the previous diagnosis of PTSD. They said they wanted me to see *their* doctor!

"It was *your* doctor who gave me the diagnosis!" I replied.

It was starting to feel like harassment. I'd first seen my personal physician, Dr. Reid, who'd agreed with my therapist and approved my time off. The department then insisted I see a physician of their choice. I suspected they'd done that when they didn't like or didn't trust Dr. Reid's diagnosis. And when they didn't like the answers and decisions from their own doctor, they forced me to see another doctor.

The appointment was set. They brought in a doctor from a town four hours away to evaluate me and decide if I really had PTSD. Repeatedly, I had been told that I was making it up, milking the system, or making a big deal out of nothing. This attempt to reverse the decision of their own physician felt like another attempt to invalidate what had happened to me. I began to wonder what rights I had and contacted an attorney.

That attorney came through my union at work. He was less than helpful. "You don't have any kind of case!"

he screamed over the phone. If he explained why I didn't have a case, I didn't hear him through his yelling.

When I contacted the doctor who gave me the diagnosis and told him what was happening, he gave me the name and number of his personal attorney and told me to call him. I did and was told that I didn't have a case because the state of Wisconsin did not recognize psychological trauma as disability. He said I should go to the evaluation, but if that doctor denied the PTSD claim, I had no recourse. There was no appeal.

I went to the appointment. I answered his questions. In the end, he agreed I was suffering from PTSD. I felt validated.

There was a small, and I mean small, disability check that came with a work-related disability. Beyond that, I had no idea what a 5 percent disability meant in my life, other than two independent doctors had said I wasn't making it all up.

One morning when I came out of my bedroom, Brenda was on the phone with her mother. She moved the phone away from her mouth and began arguing with me. I hadn't said a word. I stopped dead in my tracks, said nothing, walked back into my room, and packed a duffle bag. That was it. I walked out the door without saying anything.

My friend Tom let me stay at his vacant lake home, and I was grateful for that. I returned home to feed and care for the horses while I looked for a more permanent place to call home. A friend of a friend who had horses also had a basement bedroom I could rent and room for my horses. I now had Brenda's horse as well as my own because Brenda had threatened to sell her horse if I didn't buy him. "That horse ruined my fucking life," she kept repeating.

She seemed to have connected our getting horses with the disintegration of our relationship.

I was grateful for a place to call home, even if it was in a woman's basement. My horses had a safe home. I had help with their care when I was at work for twenty-four hours. The rent was cheap. But after a few months it became clear that I would need a place of my own. I needed my own space.

Brenda and I eventually came to an agreement on a buyout price for my portion of the property. She believed she would be unable to afford to stay there if I insisted on the fair market price for the property and cried about how much she loved the land and how badly she wanted to keep it. I felt her pain. I was sad because our relationship was ending, even though I knew it needed to, and I felt guilty that I was the one ending it. I lowered my asking price. She agreed to the price and paid me out.

Shortly after the sale, she began selling off portions of the eighty acres: twenty acres from the north, twenty acres from the south, and five acres from the west. Not long after that, she lost her job at the hospital, sold the remaining acres, including the house, and moved out of state and back to her childhood home. I felt betrayed, played, and taken advantage of.

I grieved the sale of the property and home. I loved that property. The eighty beautifully wooded acres with a pond were a place of healing for me at a difficult time in my life. When the relationship was floundering, I could walk for hours in the woods and never leave my property. Being in the woods was restoration to my frayed life. And even though I'd had only a small portion of land near the house for the horses, I had created that pasture for them. I'd cut the trees, leveled the land, put up the fences, planted the seed, put up the light pole, and brought the horses home. They were my living, breathing sanctuary, my sacred place, at a time when I'd wished for death.

While I lived in the basement bedroom, I poured myself into my horsemanship education and began looking for my own place. I went back to the same real estate agent who had sold Brenda and me the eighty acres. She knew what I wanted for my new place.

We found several potential properties that had wonderful homes but were not ideal for my horses. Often, there wasn't enough acreage for me to feel secluded and safe. And because I had a limited budget, I was going to have to forego a nicer house for the land and seclusion. The land for the horses was more important than a home for me. The land needed to be open for pasture. It needed space for a round pen, an outdoor arena, and maybe, someday, an indoor arena.

In my effort to explain how secluded I needed the property to be, I told my real estate agent, "It needs to pass the naked test." She seemed a bit taken aback. I added, "I need to be able to go anywhere on my property naked without pissing off my neighbors." She laughed and understood completely.

With my real estate agent's help, I found a beautiful piece of land on Hemlock Road. It was a secluded thirty-four acres, eleven of which were flat and open, perfect for the horses. The house was situated on a small hill in the middle of the property, surrounded on all four sides by tall mature trees and hidden from prying eyes, which was just what I wanted. It passed the naked test.

Two large windows faced down the hill toward the open land. Just like envisioning your shoes in the closet of a potential home, I could see my horses grazing in the open field. The vision brought a smile to my heart.

I walked out into the field, stood quietly, and closed my eyes. I could feel my feet firmly planted on the ground, just as I knew my horses would someday. The sun felt warm on my face, and I heard the breeze gently caressing the trees that surrounded that field. Crickets and peeper toads sang their welcoming songs. For the first time in a long time, I felt certain about something: This field would soon become a safe home for my small herd. I felt a peace I had been longing for. I was home.

The house wasn't exactly what I'd dreamed of. Built in the early 1980s, it was a ranch home with a walkout basement. Apparently, it had been a cabin that had been renovated into a home. There was lots of wood, and while I love a rustic, backwoods cabin feel, there was too much wood. Knotty pine clad the walls and ceilings in the open concept kitchen and living room. But the biggest drawback for me was the fact that the basement had a wood foundation. I had never heard of such a thing. I checked with some construction friends and was assured that it would be okay. The property was perfect, and while the house had issues, I decided I could fix them.

Fortunately, the Universe had my back. The property hadn't come up on my searches earlier because the owners had it overpriced and it was out of my price range. The current owner had been promoted at work. He and his family were leaving the state and had already purchased another home by the time I saw the property. They were very motivated to sell, so they lowered the price. That price drop put it on my real estate agent's radar, and the day I asked to see the property was the first day it was vacant. They had just moved. When I put in an offer that was lower than their recently reduced asking price, they jumped at it.

I could feel my roots beginning to grow. I could feel the dark cloud of uncertainty begin to lift. I was creating a life of my own—something I had never done before. In the past, I had filled the void in my being with the presence of other people. Any relationship quickly progressed to a live-in situation. Every relationship eventually ended, and one of us had to move. And when we owned a home together, we had to break financial ties, as well as emotional ones.

Buying the Hemlock Road property on my own, with my own money, was a new adventure. I was learning how to become my own person, apart from another. I was beginning to learn who I was.

As I started to plan my move, I thought about my horses and knew I wanted them to be on the property as soon as I moved in. For that to happen, I needed permission to begin fencing the pasture before the closing date. Because the sellers had already moved, they were agreeable. The space for the horses at Hemlock was massive compared to what they had at my previous place. Before she sold the property, Brenda allowed me to remove all the fencing I had installed there, so I brought it to my new place.

And so began the multi-year development of my new property. Hundreds of fence posts were put in, some dug and some pounded. I was creating a life for my horses as I was creating a new life for me. It was exhilarating to watch my horses turned out into their new pasture for the first time. They ran, kicked up their heels, and stretched their legs. It was a beautiful sight.

18

I wanted to improve my communication with horses and learn to share my love of them with others, so I enrolled in a four-week class in Colorado with Parelli Natural Horsemanship. My goal was to achieve a high enough score to be able to move on to the formal instructor course.

Before I left, I had a conversation with Bill Armson. We were sitting in my truck in the driveway of his and my mom's home after I had taken him to pick up some medication. He and Mom had been fighting, and it seemed with each passing year, their relationship became increasingly dysfunctional. They seemed to bait each other into ugly arguments. It was never physical, but Mom said he threatened violence on more than one occasion. I was encouraging both of them to get a divorce. Neither of them was happy.

During that conversation, I made the joke that I shouldn't encourage my parents to get divorced because I was one of only a few kids whose parents were still married.

Bill looked at me with a blank stare and said, "You know there's no proof."

I was shocked and hurt. "What do you mean, no proof?"

"Proof that you're my son."

"Do you doubt it?" I asked.

"No, but there's no proof."

"Do you need proof?"

"Yes."

"Do you want DNA?"

"Yes."

Yet again, I wasn't being claimed. If he openly accepted me as his blood, he had to face some truths about himself. His reputation would be tarnished. He portrayed himself as the moral compass and savior of wayward souls out there on the open road as a trucker, and I was a secret to be kept hidden.

I was the truth of who he was and what he had done to his own wife and family. He had an affair with a married woman—my mother—for twelve years. He fathered a child with her. My mother's marriage ended in a divorce. He continued that affair with her while he stayed married for another sixteen years before he finally left his wife and moved into my mother's house. He watched another man pay child support for a child he knew was his.

My older brother asked me a question. "Bill will eventually die. Is there anything you need to say to him while he's still here?"

"No," I replied. "There is nothing to say. I left the door open for him to step through, own me as his son, and be a father. He never has. We don't have a relationship. When he dies, there will be nothing to grieve."

I knew I wanted to tell Bill it spoke volumes about his character that he'd watched another man pay child support for a child he knew was his, but I never did because I feared he would take it out on Mom. I was also afraid speaking my truth could forever slam the door shut to any potential relationship he and I might have. I stayed silent.

I left for Colorado, thinking about DNA as I drove across the country. I had no idea how to have a DNA test done, but I knew I wanted to. I was hurt and felt rejected by Bill. I wanted to have definitive proof that he couldn't deny. We both already knew the truth, and I wanted to leave him no place to hide.

Class started on a Monday. On Friday, when I called Mom's home and got no answer, I called my sister. My brother-in-law answered. "Have you talked to your brother?" he asked.

"No. Why?"

"Bill had a heart attack. They were doing CPR when the ambulance left."

I immediately called my brother. When he answered, I asked what was going on.

"He's gone."

Time stopped. Slowly, the grief began to consume me. My last conversation with Bill had been about his continued denial of my paternity, and now he was dead. He never stepped through the door I did my best to leave open. He never accepted me as his son. The only time he ever uttered the words "I'm proud of you" was the night I first confronted him with the fact that I knew he was my biological father.

I grieved, but it took me a while to realize I wasn't grieving his death. I was grieving the death of what never was. As long as he was alive, there was still a chance that he would accept me as his son and love me. Hope remained as long as he drew breath. When his breath ceased, hope ceased. I wasn't grieving the death of Bill Armson. I was grieving the death of hope.

I spoke to Mom the next day. She told me Bill was to be cremated and there would be no memorial service or funeral. I asked her if she wanted me to come home.

"No," she replied. "Stay where you are, doing what you love, surrounded by people who care about you."

I stayed.

Learning was a blur much of my time in Colorado. I had no control over my emotions at a time when I needed it. The head instructor got angry with me after I lost control of my emotions while attempting to get my horse ready for class. Instead of talking with me, the instructor shunned me the rest of my time there. Fortunately, my friends were there to support me. In the end, I did graduate with enough points to get me a place in the instructor program that was going to be held in January of the following year.

I took the program and became a professional horsemanship instructor. That set in motion many of the pieces that needed to fall into place for me to be where I wanted to be. Not only did it put me in contact with lots of horses and the humans that love them, it also exposed me to some interesting horse-human relationship dynamics.

I began to see patterns in and correlations between the communication issues humans were having with their horses and their human relationships. I also noticed that people who really loved their horses often found solace and healing from their personal traumas by spending quiet, quality time with their horses. There was a healing component to horses. I had felt it myself, and now I was seeing it in my students as well.

Often when I was with students and their horses, they shared their personal stories with me, including stories of their most intimate traumas. Sometimes we cried together. All the while, the horses helped and healed. During those tender and intimate conversations, I sometimes shared parts of my own trauma and the healing journey I was undertaking. It was because of one of those conversations that the Universe brought me a gift.

I had shared some painful details of my past with a student who would become a dear friend. Stacey had told me about the devastating loss of her husband, who was killed in a medical helicopter crash. She and her husband, Darin, were emergency physicians at a large Level 1 trauma center. Darin flew in the helicopter and Stacey worked in the emergency department. When Darin was killed, it not only left Stacey a widow, it left her the single parent of two beautiful children who had suffered the sudden death of their father.

I couldn't imagine that level of loss. It was because of those intimate conversations that a few years later, Stacey approached me with an idea and some advice.

She said she'd started a coaching training program through a company called Touched by a Horse, run by a woman named Melisa Pearce. She encouraged me to take it as well and said it was a beautiful way to heal our own traumas. She also thought I would make a good coach. I genuinely cared about my horses and students, and I frequently saw students having relationship blocks with their horses. Those blocks often coincided with blocks in their human relationships. I thought if I could help with one of those blocks, maybe the other would improve. Stacey saw that as a good indication that I cared about people, their stories, and their lives. With proper training, I could hone my skills as a professional coach and make a difference.

I was afraid of facing the traumas that were tucked safely away in the dark corners of my heart. I knew how they'd felt when they happened, but I'd done a good job of locking those feelings away internally to avoid reexperiencing the pain. I remembered the traumas but did my best to disassociate from the pain. I couldn't imagine what it would feel like when they came out into the light, and I was terrified of facing them. I had been talking about my traumas, but not dealing with or healing them. I had been sharing the gruesome stories as a sort of badge of courage. My traumas had become my identity. They were the only thing that gave my life significance. For many reasons, I believed I didn't have the strength or courage to confront them, let alone release them. I used the cost of the program as an excuse to not go.

In that moment, another familiar voice rang loud and clear in my head: the imposter. "Just who do you think you are!" it said. "What could you *possibly* have to offer someone?" I listened to that voice. I wasn't ready.

Just shy of two years later, I was going to be in the Madison, Wisconsin, area. Stacey invited me to dinner saying she had something important to talk to me about. When we met, she again talked about the coaching program. She was about to graduate after two years. She told me stories of how gifted Melisa Pearce was at helping people like me heal their traumas. Stacey cared about me and could see what I was trying hard to keep inside. She could see my pain. She thought the world needed me to be a coach and needed to hear my story.

We talked about the cost. This time, it started to sink in. I wanted change in my life. I wanted to feel better. I was suffering, and I didn't know how much longer I was going to be able to keep the lid on it all. Maybe I was ready.

Several months later, when I was going to be presenting at an essential oils class, a gentleman approached me before class. He said he wanted to talk to me after class. I assumed it was about oils. I assumed wrong.

I found Larry after class. "I hear you have horses," he said. "I'm a coach, and I help people through life transitions. I want to use horses to assist with the healing."

This sounded familiar. We agreed to meet for lunch and further discuss the possibility of a partnership. During lunch, he told me of his extensive training. He'd learned from teachers all over the world how to help people along their paths to healing following transitions such as the loss of a spouse, retirement, or job change. He'd found that horses contributed to the healing in profound and sometimes mysterious ways. He didn't have horses, and he wanted to use mine.

We discussed what it might look like if he used my horses and my place for his coaching business. It sounded intriguing to me. I was getting excited about the idea of using my horses to help others. I knew they'd helped me.

"What's next?" I asked after our lunch.

"Well," he said, "at first I thought I just wanted your horses so I could coach. Now I think *you* need to be a coach."

I had heard that same statement from Stacey. "That's an interesting idea," I replied. "What would I do next if I were going to become a coach?"

"I suggest you talk to my friend Melisa Pearce at Touched by a Horse."

I inconspicuously pulled my phone out, and under the cover of the table, I texted my friend Stacey. "Is Melisa Pearce the lady you were telling me about?"

She replied simply, "Yes. Why?"

"Wow!" was all I could say. The Universe had my attention.

A few days later, I was looking for an oracle card deck in my bookcase. The cards I wanted had animals on them and text related to them as spirit animals. When I grabbed what I thought was the deck, it wasn't. I didn't recognize it and didn't know where I'd gotten it. My only thought was that it might have been at a white elephant gift exchange at a Christmas party I had attended years earlier. I turned the box over and there, on the back of the box, was the final nudge I needed from the Universe.

It read, "Touched by a Horse" and "Melisa Pearce."

19

I sent in my application for the Touched by a Horse program. Next was an intake call with Melisa Pearce. During the call, I could tell that I was being probed and examined. She was ensuring that I was going to be a good fit in the program.

I called Stacey after the call. "I don't think she likes me," I said.

"She does. I promise."

I wasn't so sure.

I began class the following January. I had weekly audio-video class calls, and I had to complete online content assignments and meet with my own program coach, Marsha, twice a month. I also needed to attend in-person training sessions with Melisa and classmates to be coached, learn to coach, and have in-person classes. Those classes were held both in Colorado and at other places around the US.

To graduate, I needed to do more than learn how to coach using the Touched by a Horse Equine Gestalt Coaching Method. I needed to do work on my own issues. That meant I had to have the courage and willingness to dig into my traumas and heal old wounds so I could help those I'd be coaching after graduation. I needed to be able to be with them at a deep connected level without being triggered myself. That would require me to heal my own wounds. To do that, I would have to go to the most terrifying places within me.

As I prepared to go to my first in-person training, called a CORE, which was being held at Melisa's Cave Creek Ranch in Arizona, I had no idea what to expect. I knew what traumas were laid to restless sleep, buried alive in my heart. Some of them had been so devastating going in, I wondered what would happen if all the pain and sorrow came erupting forth from within me at once. I was afraid I wouldn't be able to survive it, that it would be the end of me. But I also knew what trauma needed to be exorcised first: my childhood sexual assault.

In the large, covered arena, the chairs were arranged in a circle. When Melisa asked if anyone had work they wanted to do, I raised my hand. I couldn't keep the emotions in any longer.

I sat down in a chair directly across from Melisa, and even though I hadn't yet spoken a word, tears were already welling up in my eyes. I did everything in my power to suppress the intense emotions crashing through the walls of my resistance.

I had never felt so vulnerable, raw, safe, and seen—all at the same time—as I did in that moment. Melisa's kind eyes reached into my wounded heart and waited with me as I found the words to begin the painful and embarrassing story of a man's violation of my trust and my body when I was a child.

When Melisa realized this was a story I hadn't told in depth, she assembled a group of four of my classmates. They stood shoulder to shoulder in front of me, their hands outstretched with their palms up. Melisa gently guided me through the events of my assault while I placed my hands over their hands, one at a time, to receive my words. I was to look them in the eyes and share from my heart.

Holding their gaze while I told the story was difficult. The more embarrassed I became, the more my eyes looked down to the floor. My tears flowed. At times I was weeping so much I couldn't speak. As my story deepened, Melisa moved me from person to person, each holding my hands, holding my gaze, each receiving my story. I could feel the compassion and love in their eyes.

When I was standing before the fourth person, Melisa wanted me to scream, to release years of suffering. I couldn't. My voice was frozen, so Melisa tried a different tactic.

We walked away from the group of four and stood before a large green cube made of high-density foam and covered with vinyl. Laying on top of it was a tennis racket and a pair of gloves. I was instructed to put on the gloves, and she told me how to hold the racket with two hands. I was to raise the racket straight over my head and hit the cube with the flat side of the racket. When I did, I was to make a sound.

She placed another classmate on the other side of the cube from me and in my line of sight. That classmate's role was to portray my abuser and say things to me that brought up anger, rage, hurt, and any other emotion that would make me want to beat the shit out of the cube.

I hit that cube with all I had. The sound echoed through the arena. I yelled, I swore, I cried, and yet, I couldn't scream. Something inside me was holding tight to the notion that it was not okay for me to lose control. Maybe it was thirty years as a first responder telling me I had to be the one to keep it all together. I wasn't allowed to lose my shit. Maybe I was detached from the intense emotions because I had been taught it wasn't okay to express them. Growing up, I'd been told I was too intense and too emotional—just too much. And my experiences, both as a child and as an adult, taught me that if I gave voice to the emotions screaming inside me to be released, people would be repulsed. Or leave. Or both. I believed that to keep people in my life, I couldn't say or do anything beyond their comfort level. No outbursts, because that would upset others. No appearing to be out of control. Keep everything bottled up inside to avoid making anyone uncomfortable. I believed I was responsible for the emotional states of those closest to me, and if I molded myself to protect them, they wouldn't push me away.

Of course, all of that meant I couldn't be myself. That day with the cube, I couldn't let loose for fear of rejection.

When we finished, Melisa had me connect with everyone who had played a role in supporting me in this particular exercise (called a "piece of work" in the program). In the case of the person who played the role of my abuser, I needed to see them as my classmate and not as the person who said really awful things to me in the attempt to provoke intense emotions. I appreciated them all and felt supported by them.

As I quietly walked back to my chair, I was aware that I was looking at the ground. I was struggling again to make eye contact because I was ashamed and embarrassed. During that piece of work, the other students faded into the background. I wasn't aware of their presence. Once I was finished, I was acutely aware of their presence, and I was embarrassed I had shown that much emotion in front of others. It took me several minutes to allow those emotions of shame and embarrassment to flow through me.

It also helped to see other students do their own work with Melisa. Most of them found the tormented and wounded places in their hearts during their session. I wasn't alone in my pain. We all had deep wounds we were bravely working on to lay them to rest.

We finished our four days of training and I returned home. There were books to read, reports to write, classes to attend, and homework to be completed. The certification training was a two-year program, and it was an intense two years. Over the course of the program, I traveled to eight in-person trainings, some of which were in Colorado and some in Arizona, Illinois, and Virginia. Each class built on the last, deepening my ability to coach others while also clearing my own personal traumas from the depths of my soul. I could feel myself healing. I could feel myself growing.

I was becoming more emotionally centered. I still felt all my emotions, some of them even more intensely at times. I was also becoming aware of my emotions sooner. I could feel them in my body and then pause. And I was learning to respond rather than react. Most importantly, I was finding the confidence to kindly and respectfully speak my truth. I was learning to set emotional boundaries in my most intimate relationships.

My relationships with my daughters were improving. We were having more frequent contact with more open and honest discussions. I had never felt closer to both of them. They were allowing me the opportunity to grow and change while continuing to be in relationship with them. And they were allowing me to be in a deeper relationship with them.

I had seen many people carve family out of their lives because of past hurts and never allow them back into their lives, regardless of the amount of work the wrongdoer did. And even though I'd made many mistakes with my daughters over time, they didn't do that. I was incredibly grateful for that and for our growing closeness.

Near the end of my second year in the program, I was offered an exciting opportunity. Melisa had agreed to have a documentary film made about Touched by a Horse. She asked if I wanted to be a client in the film, and I jumped at the chance.

The film agency was a television production company based in New York. There were six participant clients in the film. Two were students, two were graduates of the program, and two were not associated with the program at all and completely new to the Gestalt work. The film crew was kind. They did their best to not interfere with the work we were doing while capturing the power and intimacy of our stories. At times, the raw emotions expressed were very moving for both the participant clients *and* the crew.

Prior to coming to Colorado for filming, Melisa asked if I had any pieces of work around my job as a firefighter that we hadn't done in class yet. One stood out. I hadn't done any work around the car accident that had claimed the lives of my two friends.

As the cameras rolled, I again sat in front of Melisa and in the presence of the other participants. Our chairs were just outside the round pen. Inside the pen and alert to our presence was Melisa's ten-year-old Gypsy Vanner horse, Rua Prionsa (known as Pri). Intense emotions immediately began to push forth from within me. It was like needing to vomit and being unable to keep it down. It was coming out whether or not I wanted it to.

I bared my soul in an effort to rid myself of the suffering and sadness I had carried with me for so many years. I shared a nightmare I'd had just before coming to the filming. The grotesque images I was shown in my sleep were unquestionably associated with the deaths of my friends, and they were my body's way of telling me there was more grief to be released.

In the presence of loving friends, compassionate strangers, a beautiful horse, and cameras, I allowed the agony I had repressed to come flowing to the surface. I allowed my pain to be laid bare in the light to be healed.

The death of my friends had kicked open the door of my world like a bully with an agenda, and over the years, it had given birth to an onslaught of symptoms within me that I had never experienced before, including incredibly graphic nightmares. I felt isolated and alone, as if no one on earth could ever understand the depth and the sharp, cold, steel edge of my suffering.

In the months following their deaths, I was often unable to sleep because I couldn't shut my brain off. When I did sleep, I had flashbacks of what I had experienced. I was irritable and moody, and I questioned if I had what it took to be an EMT. But I was unable to share with my coworkers how I was feeling.

Days had blurred and blended together. I often lost time. And I cried—a lot. Many times, I found myself curled into a ball on the floor, wailing and moaning. I suffered in silence when I was with others and I suffered out loud only when I was alone. Seemingly out of nowhere, rogue tidal waves of emotion often hit me. At times I tried to share how I was feeling, but I could see on the faces of the receivers of my words how uncomfortable they were. I learned to keep my grief to myself.

In the arena with Melisa, I was finally able to share my experience, my grief, and my emotions out loud with all their intensity. It was liberating. Melisa and Pri held compassionate space for me as I put two important parts of myself back together.

In the early morning hours when I responded to the accident that took the lives of my friends, two parts of me were present: One part was a well-trained first responder in a uniform and safely behind a wall of armor. The other part was a human being, a friend, a coworker, and a lover. That human side of me was never able to fully step into the shock and horror of what was happening before me. I had to remain in my uniform—my armor—because there was a job to do.

Melisa gently unpacked the events and my emotions. For the first time in many years, I stopped judging myself for not being able to save the lives of Terri and Tom. In that moment, I stopped condemning myself for feeling the intense pain of the senseless accident and the tragic loss of lives. I stopped condemning myself for being a human being with human emotions. I began to see that I was not weak for having and experiencing my emotions. I stood in an arena with a twelve-hundred-pound equine represen-tation of my wounded heart and allowed myself to grieve.

He took my pain without assigning blame or criticizing me for being emotional, weak, or in the wrong profession because the pain of loss got past my armor. As I placed my hands on Pri, I felt the strength of his body and the softness of his coat at the same time. And I realized that I could have the strength of character and the softness of heart to do a job that required both.

I made a difference with my patients because I had strength and sensitivity. Pri reminded me that my ability to *feel* my patients was one of my greatest gifts. Feeling wasn't a curse, as I often thought it was. Feeling was not a reason to be disqualified from a career I felt compelled to do. Feeling didn't have to reduce me to ash as the price I was required to pay to fulfill my calling as a firefighter and paramedic.

The accident that cut short the lives of my friends did have a profound effect on my life. It was a foundational brick that led me to Melisa Pearce, Touched by A Horse, Pri, and Equine Gestalt Coaching. It was a seed that eventually grew into my desire to become an Equine Gestalt Coach. The car crash had been unfinished business within me for years. I did my job that early morning as a professional, and then I denied my very human pain about it by strapping on armor and wearing it 24/7.

Weeks after my session with Melisa and Pri, I realized that my soul had paid a price for what I had seen as a first responder. That price was not paid because I *felt* the agony of loss and regret but because I had denied myself the freedom to *express* that agony. I'd held the agony in.

Holding on tight to what needed to come out had fragmented my soul.

My strategy had been tied to the misguided judgement that if I showed pain, I was weak. And if I was weak, I was in the wrong profession. It was an old-school belief mandating that I wouldn't have what it took to be a firefighter if I felt the pain of death and loss, and certainly not if I expressed it.

At times in my career, it felt safer to end my life than to publicly express my pain. To admit to my coworkers that the job was getting to me would have been worse than death because I felt I would have been ostracized. If I died stoically at my own hands, I would die a hero and not a burden to those I loved.

My session with Pri released all that pent up despair. The multitude of emotions didn't come out repugnant and contorted like I feared they would. Instead, they came out as they would if I were an injured animal, afraid and hurt. They had now been beautifully set free.

After my session with Pri, I was able to find closure to the most painful events of my career as a firefighter and paramedic. Melisa and Pri brought into focus my role as both a healer and a human. I was able to see that my contribution to my patients and coworkers was to be a light in the lives of others—a gift, just as Pri and Melisa had been a gift in my life, thanks to my work with them.

Melisa helped me see that I was honored to be there with my friends in their final moments on Earth. That was why fate put me at that scene. They didn't die alone. They died with a friend who cared deeply for them. It was the most precious gift I could give them.

It wasn't the last time I was given the opportunity to be present when a loved one passed.

Mom lived alone in her own home after Bill died, but after a while, she decided she didn't want the responsibility of maintaining her own home and yard, so she moved into an independent living retirement complex.

All of Mom's closest friends had died years earlier and she was lonely. When I visited, she frequently talked about her marriage to Dad with a sense of longing, regret, and sadness. Like many people, with the passage of time, she had forgotten the bad and only remembered the good in the relationship.

Mom was beginning to show signs of dementia—repeating questions and forgetting things. During one visit she asked me if I had ever seen Robbie's horses. I chuckled. "Mom, I *am* Robbie," I said.

She laughed and replied, "Oh, that's right."

One day Mom collapsed on the floor while attempting to get to the bathroom. She'd contracted norovirus and was very sick. Because her facility was only independent living, she wasn't found for two days. The difficult decision was made to move her to a memory care facility where she could have more help and supervision.

Mom's memory continued to fade. She knew who I was when I visited her in her room, but if she was in the hallway when I arrived, I was a stranger. It was hard to see the once vibrant woman with a wonderful sense of humor slowly descend into a shell of what she once was. I missed my mom, even though she was sitting right in front of me holding my hand. Despite all the events she'd handled so poorly when I was a child, she was my biggest fan. I had been hurt by her decisions, but I knew she never did anything to intentionally hurt me.

The more I learned about my past and its effect on my mental health, the more questions I had about her life and what had led her to make the choices she'd made. But whenever I asked a question, she replied, "I don't know." Then she quit speaking. If she liked something, she'd give me a thumbs up. If she didn't like something—like trying to keep her from eating too much chocolate or wanting her to drink more water—she simply stuck out her tongue like a petulant child.

One evening my sister called, upset, saying she thought there was something wrong with Mom. I immediately went to the memory care facility. When I arrived, she was peacefully asleep in her bed but awoke when I entered her room. I talked and she smiled. I asked if she was feeling okay and she replied with a warm smile and thumbs up. She smiled when I said I was going to head home and let her get back to sleep.

"I love you, Mom," I said, as I always did, as I left her bedside.

"I love you too," she replied.

Those were the last spoken words I ever heard from my mother.

It was only a few weeks later that I held my mother's hand for the last time as she peacefully slipped from this life. Surrounded by family, she was gone.

Six months following my mother's death, I finished my training at Touched by a Horse. It had changed my life. When I stepped onto the arena dirt for the first time, I was ready for growth. When I graduated from the Equine Gestalt Certification program, I realized I had only just begun.

20

I graduated in January of 2020. In just a few weeks, the world would stop and hold its collective breath. As a society, we didn't know what to expect. It was a challenging time for the world, and a challenging time to begin my practice as a coach.

Up until that point, I had only coached in school. Because I wasn't able to immediately begin coaching in the real world, I began to doubt myself. I knew I needed to find clients, people to coach. Where they would come from was the question.

Of the many lessons I have learned from my life, one I have used over and over again is this: When I desire something, all I need to do is put it out to the Universe. I have a specific way that seems to work for me. The words are these: I know [my desire] will happen. I just don't know what it's going to look like to get there.

I have a definite knowing, as well as a clear sense of *allowing*. I believe allowing is important because often, the Universe knows better than me how the path to the destination will look. If I try to force the path, the Universe says, "I can't supply that in that way!"

Starting my coaching practice was no different. I knew I would have a practice. I knew I'd have clients. I didn't know exactly where they would come from.

One person the Universe put on my path was Michelle. When I saw Michelle's Facebook Live post, I knew instantly who she was. Not only did she have a very recognizable name in my area, she was heavily involved in the horse world. She was someone I contemplated reaching out to when I became a horsemanship instructor in 2011. She was married at the time and had a beautiful riding facility at her home. I thought maybe I could teach out of her barn. But I was a bit intimidated by her. I knew she was an accomplished dressage rider, and I didn't feel accomplished as a horsemanship instructor. I was new to it, teaching basic horse communication skills to people. Fear prevented me from reaching out to her at that time.

Nine years later, I saw her social media post announcing that she was in recovery with four years of sobriety, and she was about to open a sober home for women who were coming out of treatment and/or were new to recovery.

I saw a possible collaboration. By digging into my traumas and doing a lot of personal work, I had grown and healed. Because of this, I was developing confidence in my abilities as a coach. She was going to have the clients I wanted to see. I was also impressed by her courage to post on social media that she was in recovery.

I sent her a message expressing my desire to assist her in her efforts with her new venture, but I was vague. I didn't tell her exactly what I did.

She quickly responded and asked what I did that might be of help. I told her that I partnered with horses to help people heal the traumas of their past. She wanted to know more. She later told me that when she read my response, she laughed out loud. The treatment facility she had been through had used horses, and that was a treatment modality she wanted to incorporate into her sober home. And there I was, offering horses to heal trauma.

A few weeks later, I was going to be teaching horsemanship at a barn I'd taught at monthly for several years. Holly was a perfect host for me. We would schedule the dates and she would do all the work of lining up the students and scheduling their time slots. All I had to do was show up and teach.

Holly knew Michelle and somehow knew I'd been talking with her. She invited Michelle to come out when I was going to be teaching and meet me. The day Michelle and I met at that training changed the momentum of my business.

"What is it that you do?" she asked with sincerity and kindness.

"I'm an Equine Gestalt Coach," I replied with all the confidence I could muster.

"What is Gestalt?"

That was the question that could strike fear into the heart of a newly graduated coach. I did my best to put into words something that was best felt. I explained that Gestalt is about being in the here and now, exploring our lives rather than defining them. I told her that the answers a person was seeking were already within them but outside their awareness. As a Gestalt coach, my role was to set up an experience that allowed the person I was working with to bring forth their own answers. By using experiences to explore their inner selves rather than simply talking, profound discoveries could be made.

"We have some time this morning. Gestalt me!" she said.

Because I had graduated from the Touched by a Horse Equine Gestalt Coaching Method program right before COVID hit, I'd been unable to coach clients face-to-face for some time. So when Michelle asked me to coach her, I had never coached a client in person except during my training experience. Inside, I was panicking. I knew it was a job interview. On the outside, I put on my best poker face, combined with my I'm-about-to-run-into-a-burning-building face. I got this, I told myself.

I used Holly's horse, Emera, for my session with Michelle. I was familiar with Emera and her temperament, but I had no idea how she would show up in a piece of Gestalt work.

As Michelle, Emera, and I made our way to the round pen, the other people at Holly's barn that morning for the horsemanship class began to gather outside the pen. Not only was I having a job interview with an influential woman, I had an audience. I had spectators for my first ever Gestalt coaching session.

Within a few minutes of exploring with Michelle, I was solidly in my coaching zone, and it was clear she had two parts of herself that were having a dialogue about her opening a sober home. One side of her felt confident in her decision and her ability to be an effective business owner and positive role model for the women who would be at the house. The other part of her doubted her ability and was the voice inside her that spoke limiting beliefs: *Who do you think you are? What makes you an expert? Why should anybody listen to you?* Of course, they were the same limiting beliefs I had. The same ones many of us have.

As Emera roamed inside the round pen with us, I placed a wooden pole on the ground and encouraged Michelle to have a conversation with each side of herself: the side of herself that was confident and the side that doubted. She did a beautiful job of staying in the moment and courageously explored the point that each side was making.

As she began to make peace with each side, Emera began to move closer and closer to us. Earlier, Emera had been uninterested in what we were doing and was grazing. Now she was becoming more invested in what was happening. When Michelle became more centered in her place of confidence, Emera moved in close. Finally, Emera stood directly across Michelle's path, blocking her return to her unconfident side. Emera gave her the answer: Stay in your belief that you are capable, confident, and on the right path.

Michelle was impressed. In that moment, she was a believer in Equine Gestalt Coaching and a believer in my ability as a coach. I had a referral source for clients.

I began seeing the ladies at Eau Claire Sober Living as clients. Michelle was an advocate of my work and my abilities at helping others heal. She encouraged her women to have sessions with me.

When the weather was pleasant, I saw clients at my house and partnered with the horses. But sometimes the weather turned and appointments had to be rescheduled. I needed a healing space out of the elements. I needed a building.

It was not a great time to be planning a major construction project. We all thought the end of 2020 meant the end of COVID. It didn't. The pandemic had become endemic. It was never going away. With its recalcitrance came other issues, like a shortage of building materials. And what was available was extremely expensive. A four by eight sheet of plywood cost about $13.00 before the pandemic. As I was pricing building materials in 2021, that same sheet of plywood cost $48.00.

There was no guarantee that prices would come down. I had to move forward with my project, and I began putting ideas to paper for a building layout. I sought advice from people who had indoor riding arenas, asking as many questions as I could think of: What did they like about their building? What didn't they like? What would they have done differently?

I also had a dear friend who did design work for a living, and she agreed to help me with a design I could take to a builder. She put a lot of her own time and effort into design ideas. As we dreamt about everything I wanted for my business home, it became clear that I was going to have to scale back my grandiose ideas because I couldn't afford everything I wanted.

As I formulated my business plan, I also did my best to manifest the money needed for the project. Not only had COVID impacted the availability and cost of building materials, it had led to a surge in home prices. I had made a sizeable down payment when I bought my home and had lived in it for twelve years. I thought I could refinance my home and get more than enough working capital.

I applied for a loan and the bank sent an appraiser. The numbers didn't come in as I had hoped, and the size of the building needed to be cut back more. I was fighting off feelings of defeat. I had a few clients coming to get help but not enough to pay for what I was planning. I had a vision of what I thought my business, named The Heart of a Horse, could be. But it was only that—a vision. If I refinanced my home to the maximum allowable amount and my business failed, I could lose my home.

Through friends and their recommendations, I found a builder from our local Amish community who could help me for a reasonable price. Mervin had a reputation for quality, and he knew what it took to erect a structure of the size I needed. That spring, Mervin and I signed a contract for the construction of a building just over eight thousand square feet. Work would begin that summer.

The availability of materials for other projects Mervin was on began to push into my project, creating delays. When we began ordering materials for my building, there were more delays. Summer turned into late summer, which turned into fall, which turned into winter.

Construction of the home of The Heart of a Horse arena finally began at the beginning of December, and I couldn't have been happier. I felt an air of confidence wash over me. Building this arena was the right decision for me and my business. Failure was no longer in sight.

I began sharing the progress of the construction project on social media. I wanted my contacts to know that my coaching business was growing. I also wanted a visual record of the project to be able to look back on in the years to come. It was heartwarming to see the responses to my posts. People were watching, and it was exciting.

By the middle of December, all the trusses were up. I was set to leave on a vacation out of the country, and high winds were forecasted. Mervin put in some extra bracing to help hold the arena up. There was no sheeting on the sidewalls or roof to add stability. It was probably the worst possible time for high winds. Having all the trusses in place made the building top heavy.

The winds blew. My friend Paul, who did excavation work and was helping Mervin during construction, stopped by in the evening following the storm. He'd fully expected to see that the building had collapsed, but by the grace of God, my building was still standing.

When I returned home, I was relieved. Upon close inspection, I found that several of the extra bracings were broken, twisted and snapped by the force of the wind. Mervin told me that the building had been pushed out of square by the wind. Much like my life, outside forces had tried to knock it down, but it had withstood the assault. It was rocked but not destroyed. Like me, it remained standing.

As my building neared completion, I was writing the final checks for construction. They were large checks, the size you have to write smaller so all the zeros fit in the tiny box. Inside me was a gnawing and growing fear.

Imposter syndrome was pounding on the door of my heart again, doing its best to beat me down. I had invested everything I had into my dream, and I had posted all over social media about what I was doing and the business I was starting. I could no longer fail in private. If I failed, my naked in school dream would be real. Everyone would know I had not done what I said I was going to do. Everyone would know I had failed. I felt completely exposed.

I shook hands with imposter syndrome, acknowledged his presence, and asked him to take a seat. I continued on.

I saw my first client in the new home of The Heart of a Horse in the spring of 2022. Building a home for my business created a safe place for clients to come to, and come they did. Slowly, belief in myself began to grow. Clients were returning for follow-up sessions. I was beginning to see that I was providing value to those seeking help.

21

My healing has been underway my entire adult life, whether or not I have been conscious of it. The Universe has always been working with my best interests at heart, even when I thought it was conspiring against me. At this stage of my life, it feels as though I've passed through the fire. Some smoldering within occasionally bursts into a small flame, but I'm more likely to notice the heat of it and put it out before it can swell into something bigger. And I'm not naïve enough to think that there will be no more major tests to my growth and healing ahead of me. The human experience is the human experience. My life will undoubtedly be marked with joyful experiences as well as heartaches, but my view of my life and the beliefs I choose to hold have changed. Today I choose to believe that my life is magical and the Universe always has my back.

The Universe sometimes supports us in ways that are not immediately obvious. That was the case when I felt inspired to reach out to Ted Pullman. At the time I started the process (two years before I began my TBAH training with Melisa Pearce), I believed I had sound logic in doing so. Many times in the past, I could see how another person's patience or forgiveness had allowed me the freedom to grow. I felt I could offer him the same freedom. I had started to publicly share the story of my abuse, and it was clear that by doing so, other people felt permission to share their stories, often for the first time. Something good had come from my experience. I wanted to show Ted Pullman that I had created a good life in spite of what he had done to me. I wanted him to know that if he was harboring any guilt over what he had done to me, he could let it go.

I also wondered if he might be interested in joining me to create something healing for others. If he was receptive to a conversation and we could find some sort of closure to what had happened between us, maybe he would be interested in joining me onstage in telling our story. We could educate children and parents about the dangers of sexual predators. Certainly, Ted could offer extremely valuable suggestions to help parents better protect their children. I also felt that appearing onstage together could be a beautiful example of how a horrible trauma didn't have to be the end of someone's peaceful and productive life. Ted's actions and the devastating consequences that followed for each of us didn't mean we couldn't change. I felt he and I could offer hope to others on so many levels.

I contacted an organization based out of the University of Wisconsin Madison Law School called Restorative Justice. This organization helps crime victims create safe dialogue with their perpetrators. The purpose is to create a sense of closure for the victims of crimes. Normally, these conversations occur when the perpetrator is still in prison. My case would be different because the man who sexually abused me was already out of prison.

My first phone conversation with Jonathan at Restorative Justice centered around what my case involved and why I wanted to have a conversation with Ted Pullman. I explained to him that I had done a lot of personal work around my sexual abuse and felt having a conversation with Ted was the next logical step for me and my healing. I explained that I was in a good place with everything that had happened all those years ago. I told Jonathan I wanted to tell Ted that I forgave him.

Jonathan came to visit me at my home to interview me, and when that meeting concluded, he told me he was comfortable moving ahead with my meeting request. He said it was a slow process, often taking up to a year before the actual meeting happened.

As the process began, many questions stirred within me. Did he remember what he had done to me? Did he feel guilty about his actions? Did he remember me but didn't care what he had done? Did he have some twisted justification explaining what he'd done?

When I first learned that Ted had been arrested, I called the assistant district attorney's office. I had questions and I had information. I was ready to tell authorities what happened to me. The assistant district attorney informed me that Ted had not only been arrested, he'd already been tried and convicted. They were at the stage of compiling his background for the purpose of recommending a sentence. I was assured the information I shared about my abuse at the hands of Ted would be used in his sentencing. I got more than I expected.

During a follow-up conversation with the assistant district attorney after Ted's sentencing, I learned my name had come up in court. He was given a ten-year stayed sentence for my case, which meant that if he committed another crime within ten years of his release from prison, he would not only be sentenced for the new crime, he would spend another ten years in prison for what he had done to me. If he didn't reoffend, he would not suffer any consequences for abusing me.

I was assigned a victim identification number (VIN) associated with Ted's case because I was one of his victims. I was told that because I was associated with his case, I would be informed at the time of his release from prison.

When the time came for his release, I was not notified. I happened to see it when I searched his whereabouts in the Wisconsin Sexual Offender Data Base. When I called the phone number on my VIN card, I was told there had been a mix-up when their system upgraded and some cases did not carry over into the new system. They apologized and reassociated me with his case. After that, I was notified of his address whenever he moved.

Jonathan gave me regular updates on his conversations with Ted and what his responses were. I was told Ted was very apprehensive about meeting with me and really wanted to know why I was making the request.

After six months of exchanges between Jonathan and Ted, Ted informed Restorative Justice that he wanted a six-month pause in the conversations. He wasn't saying no to meeting with me, but he wanted to wait. He said that he was dealing with medical issues and needed to focus on them.

The peaceful, forgiving place I thought I was at when we started this process instantly turned to anger. I was shocked at the intensity of the anger inside me. It had apparently been incredibly well hidden. I was angry that he'd been in charge of how everything went all those years ago and still seemed to be in charge. I felt as powerless to speak my truth to my abuser as an adult as I had felt as a child. He was in control when I was eleven years old and he was in control again. I found myself questioning how he felt about what he'd done. Did he feel guilty or even remember me?

When I told Jonathan how angry I was at Ted's halting of the process, he replied, "That's why we take this slowly. Sometimes we don't fully understand the emotions within us."

He was right.

When Ted's requested six-month pause had passed, Jonathan reached out again. Ted was still hesitant to meet, but he was at least still in the conversation. He continued to reference his medical issues and continued to question why I wanted to meet with him.

Several months later, Jonathan called and said he didn't think the meeting was going to happen. He advised me that if I had anything I wanted to say to Ted, I should put it in a letter he would send to Ted. That appeared to be the only way I would be able to say what I needed to say to Ted. I looked inside and wrote.

In my letter, I told Ted that in spite of what he had done to me, I had created a wonderful life. I had children and grandchildren. I had a great career and had purchased a home. I shared with him that I was publicly sharing my story of abuse and healing and in doing so, other victims of abuse felt free to share their stories, some for the first time. I told him that the last time he'd seen me, I'd been a child, and he had abused me. I wanted him to look me in the eye and see the man I had become.

I also told him I wanted to know more about him. Where had he come from? What happened to him that led to his abuse of children? I believed I needed to better understand him, and in doing so, I might better understand why this had happened to me. Whether he liked it or not, our lives were forever linked because of what he had done to me.

I told him if he was harboring any guilt over what he had done to me, he could let that go. I forgave him.

Shortly after receiving my letter, he called Jonathan. He would not be meeting with me. He said that after receiving my letter, he'd begun having nightmares.

I had my answer. He still held guilt because of his crimes. I felt a sense of comfort and relief that he apparently remembered me and was troubled by what he had done. I felt conflicted for finding comfort because of his internal struggle. On one hand, the child in me that had been hurt by Ted said, "Good! I hope you do suffer!" On the other hand, I hoped he could release his guilt and maybe find some peace in his own life, as I had.

Several years later, I felt the pull again to understand what had happened all those years ago during his court proceedings. I wanted to see the court transcripts. I called the county courthouse that his case was tried in. I was in store for a disappointing shock.

When I called, made my request, and gave them my VIN, I was told my name was not associated with the case. They had no idea who I was. There was no longer any record that I was one of Ted's victims. It was as if my sexual assault never happened. There was no longer any validation I had been a victim of Ted's perversion. There was no proof that I could point to and declare that this really had happened to me.

Then it dawned on me why I had been removed from the case. Ten years had lapsed since his release from prison. He would only be held accountable for his crimes against me if he reoffended in that ten-year time frame. Because he hadn't—or at least hadn't been caught—my case was expunged. He would never be held accountable for stealing my childhood.

In time, I realized that I didn't need my presence on his court case to validate what had happened to me. I did that for myself. I no longer needed to drag the anchor of that trauma behind me like a badge of courage. I had accepted the fact that it had happened to me, and as a child, I'd done the best I could. I could stop punishing my inner eleven-year-old for not telling Ted no and for not telling anyone that he had abused me.

Like many things in my life, I could drop the meaning I had assigned to the events of my assault. I had squeezed as many life lessons as I could from my abuse. What remained was waste that didn't serve me and could be discarded.

I let the rest go.

Lately, the Universe has afforded me many opportunities for growth and self-discovery. The journey has been a colorful carpet laid before me upon which has been spread joy, laughter, pain, and sorrow. That is the human condition. In the past, I did my best to lean away from, avoid, and run away from any of the emotions I would label as bad. Today, I do my best to lean in to them because life has been teaching me that the place where those negative emotions reside is where my greatest lessons are born. And ultimately, the lessons bring me peace, joy, love, and laughter.

I've learned that life is about contrast. In the past, I wanted joy and not sadness. The truth is, I can't have one without the other. In the past, I chased the light and avoided the dark. I now know that without darkness, there is no light. I would have no reference point for joy if I didn't know the weight of despair. If my desire was to authentically live a full, rich life, I had to understand and appreciate the contrasts that come with life. We must learn to find lessons for better living in the darkest of hours. Otherwise, those experiences are just dark, destructive times that were endured.

So what have I learned? What are the most important lessons from my life that I have internalized and done my best to apply? If I were speaking to my twenty-year-old self, what would I want him to know? What advice would I give him? Why do I feel emotionally better than ever before?

I have recently described my emotional state as centered. For a while, I thought maybe I would describe my world as seeking balance. I was corrected by a friend when she said there is no balance in life. I had to think about that for a while and I now agree. Life is ever-changing and it is often unbalanced. Some area of my life is often out of whack, and yet, I still feel great. Why is that? I believe it's because I have adopted a desire to be centered.

If one part of my life seems out of control and my balance is thrown off, I simply move the other way and return to center. If that side becomes out of balance, I adjust again to bring it all back into flow. I'm aware of the imbalance,

I feel it early, and I adjust accordingly. I remain centered while my base is in constant flux, as life often is.

The first step in my new center-focused life was the search for self-awareness. An old mentor once said to me, do less sooner rather than more later. He was referencing my work with horses, and it applies to my emotional health as well. To do that, I needed to become aware sooner and make a small correction rather than living in an unaware state of mind and waking up in the bottom of the well, unsure how I got there or how to get out. If I had been aware sooner, I could have walked around the hole in the ground or, even better, taken a different path altogether.

Once I began to quietly feel the minute changes in my internal system, I had a small thread to pull on to begin to unravel what was happening within me. It was the first step toward being in control of my emotions rather than continuing to be at the mercy of external forces that always seemed to be in control of my mental state.

When I felt grabbed by a negative emotion caused by some trigger, that emotional tug had to be pretty great for me to be aware of it. I might be feeling anger, jealousy, or fear, such as fear of abandonment. Whatever I was feeling, the less aware I was of it, the more prone I was to unwarranted arguments with a romantic partner, defensiveness, or some other dysfunctional behavior. I often wasn't aware of the emotion that had been triggered, and I was even less aware of the trigger itself.

I was in the infant stages of learning my newfound superpowers: awareness of my internal state and the ability to pause before reacting. I was becoming aware of rising internal emotions and how they had been directing my external reactions. At times I would still have the outward reaction tied immediately to the emotion of hurt or betrayal, but at least I was aware of what old wound within me was being triggered. From there, I needed to summon the courage to apologize and clean up the mess. Before I had the self-control to self-soothe, I learned that my insecure reactions were the equivalent of dumping gas on a fire. By paying attention to my body, I was gradually increasing my ability to feel the rising tide of emotions, often at an earlier stage, and instead of looking for the usual soothing solution in another person to reassure me that I was okay, I was learning to quiet the emotions myself.

Many of my relationships suffered, crashed, and burned because of my insecurities. I was doing the best I could with the tools I had, but I didn't know how to self-soothe. I hadn't known the source of my triggers or what wounds had been left unhealed, and I'd been relying on another person to make me feel better. I was seeking an outward solution to an internal problem. I was praying that another person could fill the emptiness within me created when I was a child, and I wanted another person to heal me. Before I learned to pause when I felt emotions taking hold of me, I often made matters worse. I was using the same problematic habits and patterns, again and again, and getting the same unsatisfying results. I kept falling into the same well without knowing why.

As I continued to learn how my inner emotional state influenced how I showed up in the world, I began to find I had some control of my emotions. I could feel the rising emotion and name it. And then the next big breakthrough came. I learned to pause. I learned to look inward when I was feeling the emotion rather than afterward. This development created less need for apologies, and difficult conversations with others became calmer. Because I was calmer, I could begin to learn the art of listening to understand rather than listening to respond. When it's brought to my attention that I haven't shown up well, I can now apologize without feeling shame. I can own my actions and make amends without defending my triggered response.

Like the block foundation of a house being built, a few bricks are placed on one side and then a few are placed on another side. Eventually, the sturdy foundation of my new life being built began to rise. I was using the training I had received at Touched by a Horse to coach myself. Like my clients, I could see when I was emotionally overreacting, and I was learning to use the red flag of intense emotion to look inward and see what was happening and what past trauma required more healing. I was getting underneath the superficial to discover the root of the problem.

PART 2:
LESSONS LEARNED

Lesson 1:

It's All a Gift from the Universe

When in the middle of the many storms that have been my life, I had no idea what lessons I was supposed to learn. I felt life was conspiring against me and that I was cursed. I thought life was always going to be difficult and hopeless because it always had been. I couldn't change the horrible events of my past or the family dynamics I grew up in. And if I couldn't change the past, there was no way to change my reactions to those events. The pain, loss, and loneliness I felt would forever be present.

I was wrong.

I didn't realize that God was working magic in my life. I wouldn't see the magic unfolding for many years. When I was in the middle of the turmoil, I needed time to pass to better understand the miraculous gifts I was receiving from the Universe.

Søren Kierkegaard once said, "Life can only be understood backwards; but it must be lived forwards." I understood that I needed to get on with my life, but to see the bigger picture, I needed to look backwards through the clarity of time. I couldn't see the path that was being laid before me in the beginning because I was too close to the heartache and pain. I needed space between myself and the events to reap the reward of understanding that would eventually create an indescribable amount of joy in my life.

With each traumatic event, a pin was being placed on a map. One pin on the map did not allude to a direction. Two pins gave a hint. I was in training and didn't know it. Three pins. Four. Looking back and seeing all the pins between then and now, I can see a clearly defined path that has led me to where I now am.

Each traumatic pin represented a growth point, a revelation, a training session that I needed and would be able to share with another, a way through the fire. Each pin was like a diamond that found its way through the pressure that created an illuminated path to peace. I had to experience what I did to be who I am today. I'm glad I didn't give up.

One of the most heartbreaking events of my young life was my first divorce. That time was like being wrapped in a heavy black blanket I could not escape from or see my way clear of. I felt as though everything was being ripped from me, and I was drowning in despair and rage.

Looking back and following the pins, I can clearly see the path. Had I not met my first wife, Amanda, I wouldn't have my beautiful daughter Danielle and my magnificent grandson. I also would not have met Amanda's foster mother, who suggested I apply for a job with the Wisconsin Department of Corrections. I did and was given a job that had a retirement account. At the time, that didn't mean much to me. After all, I was only twenty-one years old.

After the divorce, I quit being a prison guard and was hired as a career firefighter. I again had a retirement package. I didn't realize it was the same retirement account as the one I had with the prison system. All my years of service prior to the fire department counted.

At fifty-one, I was able to retire from firefighting after a combined total of thirty years. I have an incredible amount of gratitude: gratitude for my first wife, the gift of our daughter and our grandson, and the strength and wisdom I gained from those years. Without Amanda, I wouldn't be doing what I'm doing today.

My career with the fire department gave me the opportunity to purchase my first horse. Time with my horse saved my life following my diving accident. That accident opened my eyes and heart to the healing I needed, not only for the diving accident but also my sexual abuse. My retirement account, which went back to my early twenties, allowed me to retire at an early age. Being involved in the horse world put me in front of the people who would lead me to Touched by a Horse. Who I am today, including my passion for coaching and teaching, would not have been possible without that chain of events.

My marriage and subsequent divorce from Amanda were unquestionably low points in my life. At the time, I felt that I had lost everything. And because I was still in the middle of the chaos, I was unable to see what personal life lessons I would eventually gain from this dark period.

I don't know that I could have done anything to salvage my first marriage, based on who we both were at that time. I do know I did little to improve our situation. I reacted and added fuel to the fire that eventually burned down our relationship.

I've learned that bad things happen, and that life is full of events we wish would never have occurred. The joy in my life has returned because I have learned to see those bad things through a different lens. As I learned more about myself and the life I wanted, I had a choice: I could continue to view events as outside forces that had a negative impact on my life or I could look back at them and pull out the good that came from them. For instance, to only focus on the chaos during my marriage to Amanda would keep me in the space of victim. But to focus on the beauty that resulted from that relationship brings me joy rather than pain. It also gives me the ability to view my ex-wife with the compassion she deserves. She wasn't the only one in the relationship, and she had her own demons.

How are you viewing your past? Are you viewing the past events of your life through the lens of what the world or other people have done to you? I acknowledge that it can be difficult to avoid feeling like the world is conspiring against us when we're in the midst of a struggle, but when we can detach from the struggle long enough to find a few moments of peace, it's possible to remind ourselves that whatever is happening in the moment is a pin on the map of our lives and part of a larger journey that may be leading us to important learnings and growth, and ultimately, to the life we desire.

Lesson 2:

There Will Be Triggers

S o what *can* we do when we're in the midst of struggle? I do a couple of things I can recommend that help at such times: When I find myself in an unfolding difficult situation, I rely on past events that have felt similarly and remember that the intense emotions I'm feeling will pass. The important part of this is not to act or speak when I'm in the center of the intense emotions. If I need to excuse myself from a difficult conversation for a time, I do. Nothing good happens when we react while in a triggered state, so pausing when we're triggered can provide the time needed to get back to a state of mind in which we can think more clearly.

I have a good idea of how I respond to triggers: a gripping sensation in my chest, difficulty breathing, difficulty thinking, the world closing in and the need to escape, panic. For many months following my diving accident, I had debilitating panic attacks. One such episode followed being triggered at a fire department training session.

We were training with a bag valve mask, which is a device used with patients when we need to assist their breathing. Normally we practiced on mannequins. That day, we were practicing on each other. A rubber mask fits tightly over the patient's mouth and nose and a collapsible bag is squeezed to push oxygen into the lungs. The instructor asked for a volunteer to come to the front of the class and take the role of patient. I immediately volunteered. I knew I was going to have a difficult time, and I didn't want to struggle with a coworker bagging me, which I instinctively understood could be a trigger. I assumed being at the front of the class with some physical distance between me and my coworkers would somehow create safety for me. I was wrong.

I lay on my back on the table in front of the class. As the instructor was teaching, I lost my ability to hear and the world around me closed in. My chest grew tight, my heart raced, and I could hear my heart pounding in my ears. My breathing became shallow. When the instructor placed the rubber mask over my nose and mouth, it smelled like the rubber from my dry suit during the accident. And then I could no longer breathe on my own. My breath was completely dependent on him. As he bagged me, my panic intensified. I quietly started to cry, and I felt a tear begin the slow descent down my cheek. I prayed my colleagues couldn't see me crying.

One result of being triggered that day was my first experience of losing time. Shortly after the training ended, I was on the phone with a dear friend while I was driving, telling her what had happened at the training. All of a sudden, I realized I didn't know where I was. I was lost. I had ended up someplace and had zero knowledge of how I had gotten there.

I was grateful to be on the phone with my friend. When I told her I was lost, she very calmly began talking me through my growing anxiety. I told her I assumed I was on the interstate because I could see two lanes of road in each direction. I didn't remember getting on the interstate. I had no idea what direction I was going. I kept driving until I came to the next exit, turned around, and found my way home.

I was embarrassed. It had been a year since my accident. I shamed myself by assuming I should be over the accident and not have incidents like this.

My experience that day during the training session was clearly a trigger. Having the mask held firmly on my face had taken away my ability to breathe on my own, and that feeling took me back to the day under the ice. That and the rubber smell triggered a reexperience of the trauma. It was big, loud, and unmistakable.

Years later, I had another beautiful ah-ha moment about the effects of being triggered and what they looked like. The more I paid attention to my body somatics, the more my awareness of my internal state grew, and I began to feel subtle shifts. I was hearing even the quietest changes.

For years, it was as if my emotions needed to be screaming at me for me to hear them. As I healed, the rising tide of emotions could be heard as a soft voice—and eventually as a whisper.

That ah-ha happened while traveling in the car one day. I relayed a story about my father to a friend. That led to a memory of my father's wife and some horrible things she'd said to me. I felt a trancelike state come over me. I was experiencing intrusive rumination and was caught in a slow-boil response to a trigger. It wasn't big and loud. It was quieter than the others, but it was happening nonetheless.

The awareness of what was happening to me was like a bolt of lightning. I had been suffering with these brain highjackings for decades. As a firefighter and paramedic for twenty-five years, there were few places I could go in Eau Claire that didn't produce a memory of a traumatic event I had responded to. Each time I drove past a house—or in one case, a parking lot where a young man had shot himself in the head as a statement to his ex-girlfriend—my gaze would be pulled toward the setting of the incident, and the visions of the grotesque scene flooded in without restraint. It was quiet, slow, and insidious. Each time I drove past the parking lot, I couldn't stop looking at that particular parking stall. Sadness would wash over me. The only thing I could think to do was take another route, but that was simply avoiding the trauma.

I learned that I had been living in an almost constant state of emotional flooding for decades. The triggered responses were often subtle, and I didn't know how to break free from the dark cloud that so often enveloped me.

Months prior to the phone conversation that led to my ah-ha moment about slow-boil traumas, I had had a conversation with a teacher in the jungles outside of Mocoa, Putumayo, Columbia. I hadn't been completely ready to use the sage advice I'd been given, and I had resisted it.

During my ten days in the jungle learning about plant medicines and mental health, I had talked very little about my past with Shawn Chester, founder of The Native Guides, or my four fellow students. But I had shared enough for Shawn to know I had some significant past traumas. At the close of my stay in the jungle, I had a beautiful conversation with Shawn in which I opened up more. As we sat on his deck around his medicine table, surrounded by the Amazon jungle, he shared some of his insights about me. The topic of who I am and how I became who I am came up. Shawn said he didn't want or need to hear about my past.

"Robert, I know the man seated before me is strong. I don't need to know how he *became* strong." He then made a comment I needed to chew on for a while like a piece of thick, overcooked steak. "You have no past."

I felt my insides brace. A previous statement I had made replayed in my head: Who would I be without my traumas? I was holding onto them as if they were my badges of courage—proof that I was strong—because inside, I felt weak. But they were heavy. I was trying to leap for the stars with lead weights chained to my ankles.

I had unconsciously become comfortable with my constant state of dis-ease. I was always triggered, and it had become normal. I had become comfortable being uncomfortable. Who would I be if I chose to let go of the weight? Shawn was saying that it didn't matter how I'd became strong. He just knew I was. I could let my past go.

He was right. I could let it go. I realized I had been triggered by so many things, I hadn't been living in the present. It was often a subtle thing. The big panic attacks, like that moment on the table with the mask over my face, were easy to identify. But the smaller, subtler things—like the memory of something my father's wife had said that took me down a rabbit hole—were equally destructive because they were like programs running under the surface, mostly subconsciously. I didn't need to do it any longer. A sense of freedom and lightness poured into my heart.

It was like squeezing all the juice out of a lemon. I had gotten as many lessons—juice—as I could out of traumatic events. Did I need to carry the now lifeless remnants of the lemons with me, collecting them like trophies? What Shawn was saying was that I could keep the lessons and let go of the rest.

Just because we *feel* triggered, doesn't mean we *are* triggered. There's a difference. We are not our emotions. They are experienced, but they don't define who we are. When I came to that understanding, it was the first time I felt I was in control of my emotions instead of my emotions being in control of me. I was free. I could now recognize when I was feeling emotionally flooded and choose a different path.

It takes a bit of practice, but we *can* recognize when difficult situations are triggering intense emotions and remind ourselves that when we've felt similarly in the past, the intense emotions have ultimately dissipated. And we can learn what triggers us and what those triggers feel like. Once we've begun to develop those skills, we gain a powerful sense of self-direction and the ability to make choices about how we feel instead of feeling driven by our emotions.

Lesson 3:

If Our Human Needs Aren't Met, They Will Drive Our Behavior

One of the early experiences that illuminated my path on my awareness journey was hearing a Tony Robbins podcast in which he explained what he considered to be the six human needs. It was as if the doors to my internal map had been unlocked and blown open, allowing sunlight to pour in.

I'd heard the concept once before, but I wasn't ready to apply it. The second time I heard it, on the podcast, it sounded familiar and understanding flooded in, as if a light had been switched on in my mind. The podcast was titled "Why We Do What We Do." That title got my attention because I had often asked myself why I did what I did. It seemed that the more I peeled back the layers of my psyche and dug beneath the surface, the more I struggled to understand the motivation for many of my actions, thoughts, and beliefs. I felt at a loss to fully grasp the driving factors in my life.

In that podcast, Tony spoke about the six human needs he believes determine everything we do: certainty, uncertainty, significance, love/connection, growth, and contribution. Using this model, I could see that every action I took could be placed in one or more of those buckets. Those human needs were more important to my nervous system than my goals, dreams, or even my internal moral compass. I also began to see that the traumas I'd experienced had rewired my nervous system, altering the priority of my needs and how I went about meeting them. Tony's explanation of the human needs resonated with me. Knowing where the wounds were allowed me an opportunity to heal them.

Growing up in a family where I was loved but often alone, physically and/or emotionally, created a tremendous amount of uncertainty for me. Being alone and feeling lonely created a feeling of insignificance in me. I didn't think I mattered. I often explained the empty feeling within me as a literal hole, as if a cannonball had been fired through my gut. For years I felt that gaping hole every time I heard the theme song to the soap opera *Days of Our Lives*. It makes sense to me now that I equated that song with the feeling of extreme loneliness because I had been left by my family with a stranger who had that soap opera on TV, and I had no idea when my parents would return or even *if* they were going to return.

Because of my loneliness and an insatiable need to be seen, I was the perfect target for a sexual predator. I was lacking connection with my family, so when my path crossed that of Ted Pullman, I was vulnerable to the attention he gave me because he made me feel seen and significant.

As a child, I felt there was something wrong with me because of the emotional distance between me and my family. Mom was distracted, and I could feel it to my core. And even as a child, I knew there was something happening beneath the surface of my family, something dark flowing underground that was not being acknowledged. As a child, I had no idea that the deep, dark secret was, in fact, the truth about my parentage. I didn't know my father was emotionally distant from me because he wasn't my birth father and was doing the best he could in light of that.

Learning that the dynamics within my family had created wounds within me that were never addressed was liberating. Because the need for certainty and significance is deeply rooted in our humanness, I'd unconsciously found unhealthy ways to fill the holes created when I was young.

The lessons from the events of my life and the choices I made have continued to reveal themselves. As I grow and heal, the dots connect and the clarity gently flows in.

I learned that the need for significance is a human need in all people. As I reflected on the life choices and decisions I made and overlaid them with my newfound knowledge of the importance of this human need, I realized that significance was like the wizard behind the curtain, pulling the levers controlling my actions. From there, I was forced to look at where I had sought to fill the hole of insignificance unintentionally created by my family of origin.

The obvious place to look at first was the driving force behind my career choice. I found myself questioning my motives for becoming a firefighter. Yes, I loved to serve and I loved to help people, to be a positive influence in the lives of others. But why? I haven't always succeeded in my attempts to be honorable, but I saw my decision to become a firefighter as a good thing. I saw it as a chance to be where the action was. It was a way to be needed. Everyone seemed to love firefighters, so it was also a way to be valued.

And because I'd felt insignificant all my life, feeling significant was important for me. But shame runs deep within me, and I wondered if I'd become a firefighter for completely selfish reasons. Was it possible that I wasn't as good a person as I thought I was? What if I was nothing more than an emotionally immature, selfish child searching for a seat at the big kids' table? I needed to know that my life mattered, and I feared I might have chosen a career to prove I was important to myself and everyone else.

Eventually, I came to peace with the fact that I had chosen a noble career that *did* make me feel I was making a difference in the world. And the truth was, I *was* making a difference in the lives I touched. I didn't need to have shame for feeling fulfilled with my career choice. Someone once asked me if I thought Mother Theresa felt good inside when she did her beautiful work. I had no idea, but if she did, that didn't make her a selfish person.

On my path toward healing, it also became painfully clear that following my SCUBA diving accident, I was telling the story of the accident as another way to be significant. After the accident, I felt lost, and I quickly realized that being trapped under ice was an innate fear for everyone. I told my tragic story to anyone who would listen. They would wince when they pictured themselves stuck beneath the ice, unable to breathe. Inside, I didn't feel significant, but at least I had significant trauma. I realized that I was using my trauma as a way to feel important. Something horrible had happened to me, and the reactions of others to my accident fed my need to be seen. I was using those people and their reactions to feed my ego and fill an empty place within me. Once again, it was an external solution to an internal problem. But of course, the sympathy of others never filled the vacuum. I needed to fill it myself.

The need for significance reared its ugly head in my intimate relationships as well. In that realm, it was coupled with two other powerhouse human needs: the need for certainty and the need for connection.

For me, intimate relationships have historically been triggering. I've learned that I have an anxious attachment style. I don't say that as an excuse for my behavior, and I acknowledge I didn't show up in the most vulnerable of places with a strong sense of centeredness or confidence.

As a child, my nervous system determined that people would leave and might not come back. People would befriend me and use me for their own pleasure. It came down to a matter of trust.

For children to grow into emotionally healthy adults, they need to feel safe, comfortable, and secure, as well as have predictability in their lives. That is the definition of certainty. As a child, I was loved. That was not the problem. The problem was, I didn't feel safe. The anxiety created by my childhood experiences revealed itself in all my relationships. Inside, I was terrified that the most significant people in my life would leave. If there was any type of distance, emotional or physical, my nervous system didn't believe I could be safe and secure. And when I felt unsafe, I put up walls to protect myself because I felt significance and certainty evaporating before my eyes. That method of self-protection kept me from having the closeness in my relationships I desired. I was pushing my partners away because I was afraid they would leave. With my armor firmly in place, I would react to the rising conflict feeling defensive and panicked.

In my adult relationships, I anxiously wanted to be as physically close as possible with my partner. I also needed to feel a strong emotional bond with them. That was how I felt safe. Those were the things I wanted as a child and didn't receive. When my partner pulled away, I became scared and leaned in more. I was attempting to recapture what I perceived was leaving. The more anxious I got, the more they pulled away, emotionally and physically.

The more they pulled away, the more unsafe I felt. I was searching for certainty and significance.

If *we* were not okay, *I* was not okay. If *she* wasn't okay, *I* wasn't okay. I wasn't okay unless someone *made* me feel okay.

We have to learn that we're in charge of our emotions and believe it. It's part of the human experience to feel the full range of emotions. We all want the good emotions—happiness, love, joy—but we do our best to avoid emotional pain, sadness, guilt, and grief. We medicate them with prescriptions or addictions in our attempt to push them away or distract ourselves. We need to know we're okay even when we're experiencing pain or sadness. Grasping that we are significant and that our world is safe, even in the midst of sorrow, is a muscle that requires exercise.

That was a difficult concept for me to wrap my head around. I had been told by countless people that I was in charge of my emotions. They told me other people could not *make* me feel anything and that how I felt was *my* choice. I would get frustrated when I heard it was simply a choice. If my nervous system perceived any physical or emotional distancing from people, I felt insignificant, like I wasn't important to them. And when that happened, my sense of certainty evaporated.

When I learned that not having my human needs met was the source of my negative emotions, it wasn't a big leap to understand why I attempted to fill the voids in those needs the way I did. From there, I could see that I had to fill those needs myself rather than rely on others to do so. My awareness gave me the ability to pause when I felt the old emotions rising, and that gave me the space to look inside and choose differently. Once I learned to pause, I found I did in fact have a choice. I could see that my emotions were coming from a place of wounding, and I could choose to act differently. Instead of lashing out at another person, I could take a deep breath, recognize I'd been triggered by my past, and not respond in an inappropriate way. I was finally liberated.

If we have any hope of regaining control of our internal emotions, we first need to understand that we have needs begging to be met. Once we understand that everything we do, positive or negative, is driven by our needs, we can separate ourselves from our emotions. We can view the rising emotions much like a movie we are watching rather than being *in* the movie. We are not our emotions. We are experiencing emotions. Quite often those emotions are coming from a place of past wounds. Dig deep within yourself and uncover the wounds. Finding them is like finding gold buried deep beneath the surface.

Just as the word implies, feeling and acting defensive is a reaction to an outside influence that abruptly impacts us when we feel threatened. Maybe it's our sense of significance that is being challenged because someone didn't treat us the way we feel we should be treated. Maybe we believe it's our sense of certainty that is being eroded because an intimate partner is emotionally pulling away from us. That same partner pulling away leaves a void in the fulfillment of our need for connection and can create a large dose of uncertainty that we find scary.

It's our job to figure out which needs we believe are not being met. The outside influence is like the weather. We can't change it, but we can adapt ourselves to be comfortable in it.

It's not just our internal environment that is influenced by our needs. Our actions and behaviors are also driven by them. I chose a specific career because I felt significant doing it. That same job provided a level of certainty because it afforded me a decent wage so I could pay my bills. It was a crazy enough job that I didn't always know what was going to happen on a given day, so it met my need for uncertainty. It was never boring. I got to be intimately involved in the lives of my patients and my crews, so my need for connection was met. I needed to continue to learn and grow as a firefighter and paramedic to stay proficient, so it met my need for growth. And I knew I was providing a valuable service to my community, so my need for contribution was met.

One career met all six of my human needs.

What are you doing, positive or negative, that is stemming from your innate human needs? Understanding your human needs and what you're doing internally and externally to meet them will allow you the opportunity to regain control instead of feeling that the outside world is always in control of you.

Lesson 4:

Our Stories and the Facts Are Not the Same

A nxiety was insidious. It took hold of my emotions and made my mind spin. My anxiousness usually began with an event, large or small, that I didn't have all the facts about. Like a good fiction writer, my mind filled in the missing pieces. Those missing pieces were never happy, joyful fillers. They were always catastrophes. I had an expectation. Someone wouldn't meet my expectation, and I was absolutely, positively convinced I knew why. And while I didn't have all the facts, the story I made up in my mind became the truth.

Early in my healing journey, I heard about facts and stories. I was told that when facts and stories overlap, suffering lives. When I started to hear examples of this concept, I saw myself and my inner turmoil in every one of them.

As a firefighter and paramedic, I had seen people going about their daily lives until something unthinkable happened. I saw it firsthand, and I saw it more times than I could count. They said goodbye to a loved one as they left for work or school, and they had no idea it would be the last time they saw that loved one alive.

When tragedy strikes without warning, the grief experienced by those left behind is immeasurable: the loving words left unsaid, the hug that could have been longer, one last look into their eyes. Tragedy shatters lives. The undeniable fact that people can be taken from us without a moment's notice created unhealthy anxiety in me. I had to make sure my loved ones never left my presence without hearing me say, "I love you." I was constantly afraid I would never see them again. During my career, I had seen convincing evidence that it could, and did, happen to many people. It very well could happen to me.

Once I was in an intimate relationship that was not going well. We were growing apart, and that fact was eating away at me. I was convinced that I was about to be abandoned again, and it created a great deal of panic in me.

I sent her a text. She didn't respond. After an hour, anxiety rooted in fear began to rise within me. There had to be a reason she wasn't responding. I had no idea what the reason was, but in my mind, the story that had to be true was beginning to grab hold of my emotions.

The story I made up in my mind was that her lack of timely response had to be because she didn't care about me as deeply as I cared about her. Another possibility was that she had finally found another guy who—I knew—was better than me.

The story became my truth. I became hurt and angry, and I lapsed into panic mode. By the time she eventually got back to me, I was sarcastic and accusatory. My point of view was that she'd been ignoring me, which was rude and incredibly inconsiderate, and I needed her to fully understand just how bad her lack of response was hurting me.

Here's what actually happened: She left her phone in the car and didn't know I'd texted her until she got back to her car. Nothing more. Nothing I'd been anxious about was true. It was a story I'd made up in my mind, unrelated to fact.

I've learned that whenever my mind starts to run away with a story, I need to stop and think. What are the *facts* of the situation. In that case, the facts were that I texted her and she didn't respond right away. That was it. My suffering came completely from the *story* I made up about those facts. I wasn't being rejected, which was what my nervous system was telling me, and her lack of timely response wasn't because she felt less for me than I felt for her. My overreaction was unfair to her, and my triggered responses created issues in our relationship that I had to clean up.

When I realized the dynamics of story versus facts, I wasn't proud of how I showed up in that situation. I now strive to recognize when I haven't showed up as my best, most divine self. Not every thought that leads to emotion needs to lead to an action.

The body speaks first. In the depths of the reptilian part of the brain lives that part of us whose sole purpose is to keep us alive. It perceives threats, real or imagined, based on instinct and previous experiences, and sometimes without a conscious thought, it orders us to action. When that happens and we become aware of it, we have the opportunity to see that there's a fork in the road. Usually, we needn't have a strong emotional reaction and immediately act on it. We have a choice. While there *are* real life-and-death emergencies in life, our reptilian brains tend to jump in and treat many things as life-and-death that are anything but. It's our responsibility (which is really response ability) to sort out what's real and what's overreaction.

Pausing long enough to assess the situation has become a superpower for me. Where is the strong emotion coming from? I've learned that its source is where the old wound is located. It's like a giant flashing neon arrow pointing at the irritated wound that has been festering without my knowledge.

Whenever I feel the grip of a trigger, I do my best to quiet my mind and escalating emotions just for an instant. I pause. The pause is important. It allows me a moment in time to see what is happening *within* me rather that reacting to what I perceive is happening *to* me. What are the facts and what is the story I'm creating about those facts? For me, using this technique has created more peace in both my mind and my heart, and it has also created more peace for those around me.

If you think you might have a little dramatic storytelling in your own life, here's the process in a nutshell: Consider the possibility that there are times when an expectation or unmet need within you may trigger an overreactive response to the behavior of another person in a moment when you don't have all the facts. With an understanding of that possibility, catch yourself in the act of creating a story to explain what is happening before you have all the facts. Pause and notice your emotions. Ask yourself if you have enough facts to justify the story you're telling yourself. If you don't, make the choice to suspend your internal storytelling until you do.

It takes practice, but with that simple technique you create a more peaceful internal environment for yourself and more peace for those you care about, just as it has done for me.

Lesson 5:

Defensiveness in Communication Is Like Dumping Gas on a Fire

I ntimate relationships were the place where my child-hood wounds showed up the fastest. Of course, this isn't surprising. The people we allow into our inner circle have the ability to hurt us the deepest. My goal is to stand in the presence of my partner with my arms outstretched and my heart open. The danger is that being fully open allows my heart to be exposed. If my partner chooses to plunge a dagger into my unguarded heart, there is no way to prevent it. An open heart without the certainty of what will happen is the definition of courage and vulnerability.

If I'm in a relationship with my heart guarded, I'm unable to let the other person in and be fully open to them. And if I *keep* my heart guarded, I will forever live with my most desired relationships being held at arm's length because I fear being hurt. I desperately wanted close intimacy, but at the same time, I unconsciously repelled the very thing I desired.

I became aware that I had a fortress around my heart, and those walls were preventing me from having the relationships I desired. So I began to look for how I behaved when I was operating from behind my guarded heart. It didn't take long to discover how I attempted to protect myself when I felt threatened. Defensiveness had been my constant companion. In relationships, my defensiveness often led to sarcasm. I began to realize where my defensiveness was coming from: fear of being hurt, embarrassed, or abandoned. If I perceived a message from my partner that I wasn't enough—often a story I was telling myself without sufficient facts to justify it—I resorted to the habit of defensiveness and sarcasm in an attempt to defend myself.

I slanted the information I was receiving. It's as if my most difficult life experiences had created a pair of colored glasses through which I saw the world. Let's say the lenses of those glasses were red. Looking through the glasses made everything I saw red. Was everything actually red? Of course not. What if I believed at my core the world really was red and not that I was looking through tinted glasses? What if someone told me to simply take off my glasses so I could see the world differently? Depending on how deeply rooted in my belief I was, I might resist removing my glasses. I *did* resist. In my mind, I really was being attacked, I wasn't just perceiving it. Most of the time I was wrong.

Was there ever a time when defending myself was a good idea? Of course. When there was a real threat of harm. In reality and under certain circumstances, being able to defend yourself is a good thing. When I was trapped under the ice, I fought back against the reality of my situation while I was looking for my backup regulator. My safety and survival were being threatened by the ice, water, and lack of air. In desperation, I fought back to save my life until right before I went unconscious. Drowning was a real threat, not a perceived threat.

Contrast that with having a difficult conversation with a partner. Seldom in my relationships had I ever been in any real physical danger. Whenever my inner wounded child perceived my partner was disappointed with me and the threat of abandonment loomed, I felt tension within me rise and got defensive. My vocal volume increased because I didn't feel heard, and I made the argument about me and my feelings. Eventually, the argument would reach a stalemate and both of us would be triggered. Anger and resentment ruled the battlefield. Showing up as defensive and sarcastic because my brain was perceiving a threat was the equivalent of dumping gas on an already blazing inferno. Doing so never improved communication or resolved a conflict. It only made matters worse.

When I learned to feel the emotion of defensiveness in its infancy and use the pause technique, I could then name the emotion out loud. I would say, "I'm feeling defensive."

Instantly, the grip of tension would lessen. I asked myself where my feelings of defensiveness were coming from and where I was feeling attacked. Then I asked myself if I was really being attacked and considered that my partner might just be trying to be heard—like me.

My nervous system was overreacting to an imagined threat. Even if my partner was coming to the conversation triggered, my emotions were still my responsibility.

When I began listening to understand rather than listening to respond, our conversations improved dramatically. More often than not, we were both trying to be heard. When I feel as though my partner is listening to understand me, I feel I have value and am significant, and I feel our relationship is important to her as well. When we both come to our conversations from a place of wanting to understand, the temperature in the room is greatly reduced. We're showing up from a place of love. Difficult conversations became a lot less difficult.

Conflict and tension are inevitable in relationships. Before we can achieve true connection with others, we must first let go of the notion that the perfect relationship will be free from disagreements. When we say it's not the right relationship for me because we argue, we're falling into the trap and misguided belief that the perfect relationship will be free from conflict. It's not *if* we have disagreements, it's *how* we disagree.

The people in our lives closest to us have the unique ability to trigger unhealed wounds. When we're hurt or fearful, we defend ourselves. Think of defensiveness as a

wall we quickly construct around our heart when we perceive a threat. If we react to our partner from behind that
wall, we are effectively cut off from open communication.

We all know what the tone of voice and words used by
a defensive person sound like, and we know what it feels
like to be on the receiving end of that. As the receiver, we
push back against their defensive posture. A once mild
disagreement can quickly escalate to a major incident. The
words we wish we could take back fly from our mouths
without hesitation. Defensiveness truly is like dumping
gas on a fire, and what might have been a small fire can
become an inferno.

How do we avoid dumping gas on the growing inferno
of conflict? By looking inward when we feel the rising
emotions like defensiveness and using the pause technique, we can identify where, within us, we are responding
from. We have to accept the fact that we all filter incoming
information through the lens of our past experiences. By
pausing before we say something we regret, we're taking
off the trauma glasses and seeing things as they are rather
than seeing the story we're making up. We need to allow
ourselves to be vulnerable as we listen to understand
instead of listening to respond. Using the pause technique
and letting go of defensive reactions takes practice, but
every time we activate it, we become more secure within
ourselves than we ever could with a guarded heart.

Lesson 6:

Our Motivations for Changing and Our Willingness to Take Personal Responsibility Are Important

We will do more to avoid pain than to seek pleasure. I've seen evidence of this fact throughout my life. I used drugs and alcohol to avoid the emotional pain from my sexual assault. I stopped using drugs and alcohol to avoid the pain their use was creating within me and for the people I loved. The very strategy that dulled one pain was also creating despair and thoughts of suicide. I felt lost and hopeless. My life had to become so painful, I knew I was going to die if I didn't make some changes. But to change, I also needed the desire to live.

I didn't want to die, but for a long time, I didn't know any other way to escape the pain. Death seemed the only way out. When the pain within me became untenable and I knew something had to give, it became a powerful motivator for me to begin the process of healing. Was I going to fight to live or give up and die? I chose to fight to live. The intense desire to avoid pain was the motivator to not only live, but to live my life as free as possible from the dark cloud of despair and sadness that seemed to follow me everywhere.

It was the same with my intimate relationships. I used relationships to dull pain and make myself feel valued. But because I was so wounded, I furthered the pain and ended up feeling worthless because my dysfunctional patterns would ultimately end the relationship. Often, we were two wounded people doing the best we could while having no idea how to build a healthy, loving partnership.

Looking back, I also see a slow process of budding awareness and a shifting of responsibility and ownership for my part in the demise of those relationships. I came to understand that if I had any hope of having healthy, secure relationships, I had to own my part and stop blaming my partner for my emotions. I had to stop looking for my partner to soothe me and fill the emptiness within me. It wasn't their responsibility. No external solution was ever going to be the solution to my internal issues. I had to learn that I was okay on my own without an external fix. I was learning to self-soothe, and I was learning that I could stand on my own two feet and not rely on those around me to create safety and security for me.

When I was trying to change to please someone else, it never worked. I was doing my best to be a chameleon so I wouldn't be abandoned. I was changing to appease her so she wouldn't be angry or disappointed with me. In other words, I was changing for her, not for me.

I discovered my internal emotional state was tied directly to the false belief that if my partner wasn't okay, I wasn't okay. If we as a couple were not okay, I wasn't okay. To begin the process of self-soothing, we have to begin shifting the internal belief that our contentment and peace is solely based upon *outside* influences. The truth is, it's an *inside* job. We must learn that we can feel sadness, betrayal, or any other emotion labeled negative and still be okay. The two realities of "I feel pain" and "I'm okay" can live side by side within us.

My motivation for changing needed to be based on what was good for me, not someone else. I had to learn that I was okay, or would be okay, even if a relationship was falling apart. I was okay despite circumstances not going my way. That understanding became an internal form of self-soothing.

Another important aspect of self-soothing revolves around what we do, what actions we take when we're anxious or upset. For me, anxiety happens when my brain is getting hijacked. I'm up in my head and no longer in my body, which means I need to do something with my body. One technique I use is a grounding exercise I learned in my training. It's a simple and effective way of reclaiming my body.

When I feel anxiety taking hold, I stop where I am and close my eyes. If I'm standing, I feel the solid ground beneath my feet supporting my weight. If I'm sitting, I feel the chair beneath me, supporting me. I imagine there is a thick cord running beneath my feet to the center of the earth holding me firmly in place. Next, I focus on my breath. I pay close attention to the air moving in and out of my lungs, my chest expanding and contracting with each breath. I then shift my focus to any sounds I hear and individually identify them: birds, passing cars, faint music, people talking—whatever. Then I imagine looking deep within my chest, see my heart beating, and focus on each individual heartbeat. Following that, I shift to my skin and feel the temperature of the air on it. Is it warm? Cool? Is there a breeze blowing across me? Doing this helps me to feel grounded, centered, and in control.

This technique uses the five senses to return us to our bodies, but there are many ways we can return to our bodies. If I'm in the car, I'll turn on my favorite head-banging music and sing at the top of my lungs. I've been known to scream as loud as I can, preferably when I'm alone so I don't scare anyone. Sometimes I'll go for a walk in the woods and reconnect with nature. And a warm shower or bath can soothe my anxious nervous system.

The point is, there are two parts of self-soothing, the internal part and external part. The internal part is what I do in my mind: learning to pause, determining fact and story, how I talk to myself. The external part is what I do with my body. Both are important. Combined, they're powerful.

Learning to self-soothe was one of the greatest skills I acquired. It took the pressure off my partner to prop up my emotional frailty. They no longer had to manage my emotional state. That was my responsibility. I made changes because I wanted to be better, feel better, and show up in the world better.

A beautiful consequence of doing my inner work was that my relationships improved. The important part of this was that I didn't make changes for my partner or to save a failing relationship. I made changes for myself, and in turn, those changes improved my relationship. My partner felt safer and more secure. Standing up for myself instead of leaning on my partner gave her the space she needed to breathe and feel positively engaged in the relationship. I was no longer repelling my partner with anxiety she had no idea how to manage. It was mine to manage.

When I began to regulate my own emotions, it allowed my partner the space to grow. She didn't need to manage my emotions as well as her own. She was free to delve into her own traumas without the weight of responsibility for my emotions, and I became someone she felt safe to lean on when she was struggling. I began to find the illusive emotional centeredness I had been searching for. My emotional fitness was growing. Learning to self-soothe allowed me to calm and regulate my nervous system and control my emotions. I was in charge of my emotions, and that awareness allowed me to regulate them instead of attempting to fill a void by placing the responsibility for happiness and security in the hands of another.

I had finally made the decision that I was going to be happier, no matter what. That was a big motivator. I was going to make changes in my life for me. Yes, doing so allowed her space to grow, but if she didn't choose to stay in our relationship, as devastating as that would be, I would be okay. I made lasting changes in my habits and patterns for me.

When we make changes for another person, we can't sustain them because the landscape is forever shifting. We find ourselves operating from a place of reacting to the world around us rather than having agency over our lives and emotions. I was people-pleasing, and that was a trauma response. Anytime my partner shifted into a negative emotion, I got scared. It had to be my fault. It was another sign that I wasn't enough. I was being reactive to the situation rather than being proactive by learning to emotionally stand on my own. Learning to self-soothe created a newfound place of centeredness. From a place of self-compassion, I was learning to check myself: What's mine? Have I done something to hurt my partner, or was this a trigger response on her part? I was allowing her to be in charge of her own emotions just as I was taking responsibility for mine. That was a turning point.

We know we're growing and gaining emotional fitness when we shift the responsibility for our peace and happiness from an external solution—meaning outside forces must change for us to feel content—to looking inward. We're less anxious when we stop attempting to manipulate the world around us and instead focus on what we're actually in control of: ourselves.

The way out of victimhood is to be motivated by personal responsibility. Yes, people are not aways kind, considerate, or compassionate. Situations beyond our control can knock us to the ground. It isn't the question of *if* bad things will happen to us, the question is whether you react or respond when they do. Reaction is instantaneous and emotional. Response comes from a place within that is more emotionally centered and appropriate for the given situation.

The answers lie beneath the surface, and we have the personal authority to shape our own destinies. Taking responsibility for our own peace and happiness rather than relying on others is the first step toward reclaiming our lives.

Simple actions like grounding and centering ourselves when we feel the grip of anxiety retrains our nervous system. It's not easy to step away from an escalating conversation, but self-care and self-soothing are habits we can build, much like a muscle. They become our new habits, which will eventually become just who we are.

When you feel disconnected and anxious, reconnect with the earth, reconnect with your body, and reconnect with your true self. The result of taking personal responsibility for your own happiness can be profound.

The motivation for change must come from within. We have to want it more than we want the current chaos that surrounds us. We have to want change for *ourselves*, not because we want something outside ourselves to change.

When we make change for ourselves, the outside environment can change, but for it to be a lasting change, the motivation must come from a desire to be a better version of ourselves. That's the key.

Lesson 7:
We Need to Understand and Work With
Our Internal Parts

We are all comprised of many parts. What parts show up in a given situation depends largely on the role we're playing in our lives at that moment, our wounds, and how we protect ourselves. For instance, a person may play the roles of parent, sibling, son/daughter, spouse, boyfriend, boss, or employee at different times and in different areas of their life. We can think of each of these roles as a lead character in the forefront at the moment. Accompanying these roles are sub-roles we can think of as supporting actors to the lead character.

For instance, when I'm in the lead role of Father, the part of me that might be called Loving Parent shows up, and that part can be stern as well as loving. When I'm training horses, a part of me shows up that is patient. Unfortunately, that supporting actor called Patience definitely does not show up when I'm driving in bumper-to-bumper rush hour traffic. At those times, a character called Righteous takes the stage. When I find myself in a difficult conversation within an intimate relationship, the patience that shows up when I'm training horses may not step on stage to support the lead role of Boyfriend if I'm feeling frustrated or afraid. I may need to consciously call on it or call on another supporting character, like Restraint or the Listener.

The same supporting characters don't aways show up for each lead role, but once we're aware that we have these supporting characters, we can consciously call on whichever ones might be most helpful in that situation. If you're in the lead role of Parent and your teenage daughter has come home after curfew, you may need to call on the supporting character called Calm so the Rational supporting character can step forward and ask some questions to seek clarity. But if you're in the lead role of Parent and playing with your six-year-old son, your Playful supporting character may spontaneously arise. If you're lead role is that of employee and you're doing something for the first time, the supporting character you think of as the Learner might need to come onstage, but if you're in that same lead role and nervously about to enter a performance review meeting, you might need to call on Confidence.

A character who frequently shows up in my daily life is Anxiety. He is much like a toddler who persistently cries for my attention. I have tried many techniques to tape his mouth shut, but to no avail. I've tried ignoring him, scolding him, running away from him, and shaming myself for continuing to struggle with him.

As I became more centered in my emotions, I took a different tactic with Anxiety. First, I gave him a human name so we could have a civil conversation. I named him Frank. I then began to work to understand Frank and why he was revealing himself and in what situations he was continually showing up.

I soon realized Frank was showing up any time I didn't feel safe. Sometimes he was telling me I wasn't emotionally safe. Other times, he felt I wasn't physically safe. He was playing the role of Bodyguard—not a bad part to have. I discovered his intentions were good, but his delivery was lacking. The more I tried to ignore Frank or push him down, the louder he got. He needed to be heard.

I found it was best for me to acknowledge Frank's presence as soon as he showed up, yelling his warnings to me. Instead of reacting or beginning the spiral of panic, I simply acknowledged his presence. I greeted his boisterous entrance, sometimes out loud. "Frank, I see you've arrived. Do you have a message for me?" Just the act of facing him often toned down his obnoxious rhetoric, and Frank would soften.

"We're not safe," he would reply. His message was always one version or another of that.

Once again, I used the pause technique. Maybe he would say something to the effect of, "Do you see how far away the door is?" That's Frank-speak for, "Remember when you got trapped under the ice and we couldn't escape? Well, we couldn't escape now if we had to! Too many people! Door too far away!"

Then I cued the pause and asked myself if we really weren't safe. If we were, which was usually the case, I said, "Thank you, Frank, for having my back. Please continue to do so. I appreciate your help. Please have a seat. I've got this."

If I find myself in a situation where I can use the assistance of a part of self that doesn't usually show up, I can ask for his assistance. I can call him in for support. "Hey, Patience, I could use a little help here! Come on over and help us out!"

I know it may sound like a silly mental game, but it works for me. It may work for you too. Identify the different parts of self that show up in various situations and roles you play. Some of them will be related to your unhealed wounds. Some will be protective. Some will help you work through situations. All are well-meaning but not all are optimally helpful. That's why it's important to be aware of and understand your parts and have a sense of which parts may be helpful in which situations.

Richard C. Schwartz, who founded Internal Family Systems (IFS) in the 1980s, says a core tenant of IFS is every part has a positive intent, even if its actions are counterproductive or cause dysfunction. There is no need to fight with, coerce, or eliminate parts.

For me, Frank's intentions were positive. He wanted me to be safe. But the way he showed up in my day-to-day life was definitely counterproductive and caused dysfunction.

Once I stopped fighting with my parts and sought to understand their presence in my life, me and all my parts began to have a more peaceful life together.

In the past, I didn't recognize there were different parts of myself that arrived in different situations. Some of my parts were helpful and kind and others were dark and destructive, or as I say, shadow parts. They're the less than ideal supporting actors. Beginning to understand them and listen to them rather than attempting to banish them proved helpful in the overall goal of understanding myself.

Knowing I had different characters inside allowed me to find self-compassion. Each of them had a backstory. Understanding where they come from and what their intentions were allowed me to converse with them rather than fight with them.

To fully understand that we have internal parts and embrace them, we need to first understand we are whole at our core, where our true self resides. Then we can untangle the different parts, listen to them, heal the destructive forces some parts bring to our lives, and then embrace and integrate them all.

Lesson 8:

What We Tell Ourselves Is Important

The habits of my mind have gotten me everything I have—all the good and all the not so good. All the limiting beliefs I have were manufactured in my mind. I'm a product of my patterns and habits. If I wanted a different life—more harmonious, more joyful, more loving, more secure—I had to think differently and act differently. I needed to develop different patterns and habits of thought. It was just that simple, but it wasn't easy.

My limiting habits of thought took decades to perfect: I'm emotional. I believed it's just the way I am. I'm clingy and needy. I told myself it's because of how I was raised. These patterns were ingrained in my everyday life. The problem was, I wasn't getting what I wanted out of life, and I didn't know how to change my habitual thinking.

While studying with Melisa Pearce at Touched by a Horse, I began to learn about neurolinguistic programing, otherwise known as NLP. It was my first introduction to the power of the mind and its ability to change personal reality. One aspect of NLP is focused on the words we use in communicating with other people, as well as the words we use to describe ourselves and our internal dialogue.

Words are spells. If I wanted to change my reality, I first needed to transform the language I was using to describe it.

In my quest to take back control of my emotions, I needed to stop saying things like "She *makes* me angry." NLP taught me that using the phrase "makes me" was giving away my power to someone else. If I wanted to have agency in my life, I needed to use words like "I feel angry when . . . ."

Our subconscious minds are literal. They hear what we say to ourselves out loud or internally and take those statements as truth.

If I use statements like "The Universe is always out to get me" or "Bad things always happen to me," my brain looks for evidence in the world to prove those words. And it will find that proof. The more proof I find, the harder it is to shake the internal belief that the world is out to get me. That is the genesis of a habitual thought pattern.

Being mindful of the words I used began to create a new habit for how I spoke about myself and how I described the world I wanted to live in. My self-confidence began to grow. I began to speak kind words of affirmation to myself rather than words that tore me down. I began to tell myself how competent I was instead of saying I didn't know what to do.

When we tell ourselves things like "I'm a mess" or "I'll never survive this," our brain takes those statements literally and says, "Got it! We're a mess and we won't survive!" We then begin to live those statements now programmed into ourselves. Our brain begins to look for evidence to prove the newly programmed belief is true.

When I began to change the words I said to myself and to others, I began to change the programming. The dark veil of sadness that seemed to always envelope me began to thin. The warm glow of joy began to seep through.

Another way I began reprogramming my subconscious brain was eliminating negative information I consumed. We are inundated with information from the media and flooded with messages and images that tell us we're not enough—good looking enough, thin enough, smart enough—and that the world is a scary place. None of it is true, but because the subconscious mind takes everything literally, I learned that I needed to fill my mind with positive input. I cancelled my subscription to network TV and only kept a movie channel. I read positive, informative, or educational material. And I listened to podcasts that inspired me.

I start and close my day with a short meditation. I ask God to work through me, so I can be a conduit for his messages to others. Then I place my hand over my heart and repeat three times, "I love myself, I love myself, I love myself."

Doing those things helped me rewrite my old programming. For years, I thought little of myself, and the decisions I made proved that fact. I needed to treat myself as well or better than I wanted others to treat me. As I learned to be kinder and gentler with myself, I was teaching others how I wanted to be treated. I was speaking about the good in me as well as the good in the world.

I saw that I felt more peace when I spoke about the good in life. I was manifesting abundance by speaking it into existence. God was putting in my path the things I was focusing on. My words were the beginning of that focus, and what I focused on mattered.

A coaching client remarked that the Universe is always out to get her. We were walking out of the pasture after completing a beautiful session around grief. I couldn't allow the session to end on that self-defeating statement.

I pointed out a weed growing in the pasture that was easily recognizable. As we slowly walked, I asked her to point out every time she saw another such weed. She found lots of them. What she didn't notice was that I had intentionally walked her through the middle of an area filled with clover in bloom. After we passed through the flowers, I stopped. "Tell me about the flowers," I said.

"What flowers?" she replied.

"How did you miss the flowers?" I asked.

"I wasn't looking for flowers," she said.

We find what we're looking for. My entire perspective about life changed when I realized that.

"You're looking for evidence that the world is horrible and is always conspiring against you," I offered. "When you do that, I promise that you will find proof of it. But if you look for evidence that the world is a beautiful place, I promise you will find that as well. It's all a matter of perspective. You will find exactly what you're looking for. The question is, are you looking for weeds or flowers?"

Looking for the things in life to be grateful for is looking for the flowers. The more I *look* for things to be grateful for, the more things I *find* to be grateful for. The more evidence I find, the more I look. It's manifesting at its best. My life is filled with abundance. More of this—for you as well as me—please.

The words we use matter. Imagine what your life would be like if everything you said to yourself and others came true. Would you change how you speak? If we want something different, we have to do something different. Begin the daily practice of being aware of what you say. Speak only words that are kind, compassionate, and empowering to yourself and others. Look for the flowers in your life and you'll find more flowers. The world becomes a much more beautiful place when you do.

Conclusion

T he path to discovering my true self was long. A lot has happened. In the midst of turmoil, I didn't believe a peaceful, joyous life was possible. But I kept going. I'm grateful I'm still on this side of the veil, living, learning, and evolving.

Today my life is rich, full of love, and filled with passion. If you're struggling, trust me when I say, it doesn't have to be that way. There is hope.

Much of my healing had to do with looking beneath the surface and changing my perspective. I had to look at the way in which I told my story. I learned that it's my story, and I can tell it any way I'd like.

I can choose to tell my story from a place of powerlessness, that I was the product of bad luck and bad people. I can stay with the belief that my life *could* have been better if all those horrible things hadn't happened to me and that I was a victim of my circumstances.

My life was painful when that was the lens I viewed my world through. At those times, I didn't want to live. I felt hopeless. I was drowning in my life, and then I actually drowned. That single event was the turning point. From there, I began the work of healing that trauma and all that came before it.

When my friend Shawn reminded me that all of my life events were preparing me for bigger things, I realized I was much like an athlete. Athletes have to endure grueling training sessions to perform optimally. And just like any athlete competing in something big—the Olympics, the Superbowl, the Masters tournament—by building resiliency and discipline in my life, I'm living my dream. The traumas that crossed my path were *my* grueling training sessions. They didn't *change* who I was, they *uncovered* who I was.

I am living a beautiful life now, doing what I love and what I feel called to do *because* of what I went through. None of my current life would exist without my past.

How do I know I'm healing? I know because those tragic events no longer hold a big emotional charge. When I reflect on my past, the emotion is closer to neutral. The events no longer hold meaning about who I am as a person. They're just things that happened. I no longer *need* to tell the stories to feel significant.

I'm living proof there is a way through the turmoil and sorrow. There's a beautiful life waiting for you on the other side. It doesn't matter what labels you have been given. You are not broken. You are not damaged. You are perfect, whole, and complete as you are. You are resilient. You've made it this far—that's proof that you are. The answers you may be seeking are already inside you, but they may be just outside your awareness. My prayer for you is that some of those answers are now no longer in your blind spot. You are enough. We are all in this together.

There is hope for healing. To get there, you have to go beneath the surface.

Acknowledgments

The acknowledgment and gratitude I'd like to express here have to begin with my parents: my mother, Jean, my father, Rudge, and my biological father, Bill. This book is my best effort to portray my life as I was growing up and growing as a man and the lessons I've learned. We all did the best we could. You have all crossed the veil, and I know you're still with me. I feel your loving presence daily.

To my brothers Geoff and Kip, my sister, Rita, and my sister-in-law, Mary, thank you for coming to my rescue at a time in my life when I needed you most. You placed my life ahead of your own comfort and, at times, your own peace. You were, and continue to be, my soft places to land. I thank you. You saved my life. I'm forever grateful for your continued love and support.

My beautiful daughters, Nicole and Danielle, have been the inspirations for so much of the personal work I have done throughout my life. I wanted to do better, not only for me, but for you. I'm grateful for the relationships I now enjoy with you. I explored beneath the surface to heal myself and to improve our relationships. Thank you for being patient while I sorted all of this out. Please know my discoveries are not done. I have more to learn, and I look forward to the adventure. I love you guys.

Melisa Pearce, founder of Touched by a Horse and the creator of the Equine Gestalt Coaching Method, our paths crossed at the divine right time. No words could possibly express the depth of my gratitude for your guidance, love, and patience. You held my wounded heart and provided me with the tools to put the pieces of my life back together. You provided a safe environment for me to heal and grow. This book was your suggestion. Thank you for providing the inspiring nudge. The growth you started all those years ago was given breath to flourish during the process of writing.

To my editor, Melanie Mulhall of Dragonheart, thank you for your amazing patience while I fought, whined, and sometimes cried through this incredible process. I never could have anticipated the depth of emotions I would experience during our journey together. Your expertise and advice have made *Beneath the Surface* possible. Without you, I couldn't have brought my story to the light of day.

To my friend Lee, other than my editor, you were the first person to read a very rough draft of this manuscript. Your encouraging and loving review gave me the motivation to continue and ultimately finish. You showed me the value in the words I had written at a time when I wasn't seeing any.

To the ladies of Eau Claire Sober Living, past and present, thank you for your trust as we walk together in your healing. You are a constant inspiration to me.

To Mark, I'm grateful I had several opportunities to publicly thank you for saving my life before your recent passing. Your dedication that day on the ice gave me back the gift of time.

To Don, your attention to detail and your devotion to your fellow man has made every beautiful part of my life today possible. Without you, it all would have ended that day. I owe you guys my life, and I never forget it.

Michelle, you have been the safe place for me to work through so many of the lessons I have written about here. Your ever-present love, support, and encouragement have allowed me to find the solid footing I enjoy today. Thank you for listening as I struggled putting words to our lessons. Thank you for providing the space for me to grow into the man I am today. I'm grateful for your loving patience.

Royale, Koda, Beau, Sage, and Annie, my amazing equine partners, you guys were the first to show me that healing really could begin with the heart of a horse. You have brought so much joy to my life just by being you. Your spiritual presence has brought a profound sense of peace to my life, as well as to countless clients who have graced our arena. I couldn't do the deep work without you.

To Lilly, my loving Golden Retriever, you have sat with me for every word of this project. Love you, little girl.

About the Author

R obert Goodland is a retired firefighter and paramedic and the founder of The Heart of a Horse LLC. He is a dual certified coach with certifications in Equine Gestalt Coaching Method and Gestalt Coaching Method. He lives in rural Wisconsin with his equine partners. Robert uses his decades of experience as a first responder to help others who have been affected by their own personal traumas. Robert is also a sexual assault survivor and was diagnosed with PTSD following a work-related near drowning. His love of horses and people led him to his passion of walking alongside others as they heal.

Robert can be reached at theheartofahorse.com, Rgoodland36@gmail.com or (715) 215-0733.

Want more?

Robert Goodland is available for one-on-one coaching and speaking engagements.

Speaking

Robert Goodland is an experienced speaker who captivates, entertains, and informs his audience while introducing them to challenging and thought-provoking concepts. His talks inspire deep reflection and spark meaningful conversations. If you're looking for a speaker who leaves a lasting impact, Robert is available for your next event as a keynote speaker and/or for breakout sessions. Contact him through TheHeartofaHorse.com.

Trauma Specialist and Healer

As a trauma specialist and healer, Robert offers transformative one-on-one coaching and deep healing sessions. Whether you're looking to heal from past traumas or seek personal growth, Robert's intuitive approach helps you unlock your inner potential. Experience his powerful healing work, virtually or in person, Contact him through TheHeartofaHorse.com.

www.ingramcontent.com/pod-product-compliance
Lightning Source LLC
Chambersburg PA
CBHW060759120626
46557CB00001B/30